THE
CHINESE
IN
CANADA

THE
CHINESE
IN
CANADA

加拿大的華人
與華人社會

Peter S. Li

Toronto OXFORD UNIVERSITY PRESS 1988

CANADIAN CATALOGUING IN PUBLICATION DATA

Li, Peter S.
The Chinese in Canada
(Studies in Canadian sociology)
Bibliography: p.
Includes index.
ISBN 0-19-540652-4

1. Chinese Canadians – History.   2. Chinese –
Canada – History.   3. Chinese Canadians – Government
policy.   4. Chinese – Canada – Government policy.
5. Chinese Canadians – Social conditions.
6. Chinese – Canada – Social conditions.   I. Title.
II. Series.
FC106.C5L5 1988   971'.004951   C88-093448-4
F1035.C5L5 1988

The tables in Chapters 7 and 8 are based on Public Use Sample
Data derived from the 1981 Canadian Census of Population
supplied by Statistics Canada. The responsibility for the use
and interpretation of these data is entirely that of the author.

For Terence

Acknowledgements

Trina Vicq assisted in the final stages of preparing this manuscript, proofreading the draft copy and checking tables and references. Professor Man-Kam Leung, a colleague in the Department of History, provided invaluable advice on all matters related to China. I wish to thank both of them for their assistance and advice. I was very pleased to be able to work with Oxford University Press on this book. Richard Teleky, the managing editor, has shown tremendous patience and understanding in waiting for the manuscript beyond its deadline. Sally Livingston edited it with care, and I would like to thank her especially for completing the job in a short time. Naturally, I alone am responsible for whatever errors and omissions remain.

Contents

Preface

My interest in the Chinese in North America began in 1969, when I was completing my first degree in sociology at the University of Hawaii. The state's large population of Chinese, their history on its plantations, and their recent achievements captured my interest even as an undergraduate. Two faculty members, David Chandler and Lucie Chang, encouraged me to pursue my curiosity in the area of race and ethnic relations. I am much indebted to David, who first inspired me to study sociology and later urged me to go to graduate school. Through him I met Frank Vallee, who was visiting Hawaii for a year and has since become another valued teacher and friend.

As a graduate student, focusing on the Chinese in Chicago, I benefited from the intellectual atmosphere at Northwestern University. Howard Becker was the adviser of my M.A. program, and the late Robert Winch guided me through the Ph.D. dissertation. I am also grateful for the stimulation provided by Allan Schnaiberg, James Pitts, and Richard Berg.

I began studying the Chinese in Canada shortly after my appointment at the University of Saskatchewan in 1975. The academic atmosphere in the sociology department is highly conducive to intellectual pursuits, and in particular I enjoy the colleagueship and friendship of Gurcharn Basran and B. Singh Bolaria; the former is always encouraging and sympathetic to my work, while the latter is critical and sometimes cynical about it. These colleagues have inspired me in numerous lunch breaks in the coffee lounge and many exchanges in the seminar room.

In many ways, this book is the product of over a decade of research on the Chinese in Canada. While I am interested in the Chinese as a racial minority, I have also taken the theoretical position that one cannot fully understand a minority in the absence of the majority. In this sense, the majority and the minority are defined and produced by the relationships between them, and not by primordial cultures. This book describes the oppression, the survival, and the triumph of the Chinese in Canada. These experiences have taken place in a societal context, not a cultural vacuum. Hence it is just as important to understand the forces that generate the oppression and sustain the survival as the oppression and survival themselves.

The book is divided into three parts. The first is concerned with the history of Chinese immigration to Canada, beginning around the middle of the nineteenth century. The focus here is on why the Chinese came, how they were treated in Canadian society, and why a policy of racial exclusion was formulated against them. The major argument in this section is that institutional racism against the Chinese was a structural imperative, and that it had little to do with cultural misunderstanding or individual idiosyncrasies. The second part deals with the impact of racism on the Chinese community, including the restriction of economic opportunities, the emergence of ethnic business, the disruption of conjugal life, and the delay of a second generation of Chinese-Canadians. The third section focuses on the occupational achievements of Chinese-Canadians in the period of industrial expansion in the sixties and after. The theme here is the degree to which the Canadian dream of upward mobility has been realized by the Chinese and the kinds of structural obstacles they have encountered as some moved away from the traditional service sector and ventured into professional occupations.

Readers who wish to follow the sociological debate on race, culture, and inequality may find particularly useful the section of the introduction headed 'Sociological Themes of Racial Inequality' and Chapter 9. Those who are more interested in the story of the Chinese may wish to skip these materials. Throughout the book, two systems of romanization of Chinese characters are used: the Pinyin system appears first, followed in parentheses by the Wade-Giles system.

I have chosen the title *The Chinese in Canada*, not *The Chinese-Canadians*, to stress that despite their recent occupational and educational mobility, they have not been fully accepted into Canadian society. *The Chinese in Canada* conveys a sense of alienation. Certainly for most of the 130–year history of the Chinese in this country they have been alienated from the mainstream of Canadian society. Indeed, even today, in the eyes of the public, Canadians are often equated with Caucasians, while Chinese- and other non-white Canadians are frequently seen as foreigners. It would take more than a change of public attitude to bring about a truly multicultural Canada. If I should have a chance to update this book in the future, I hope I shall be able to entitle it *The Chinese-Canadians*.

I am dedicating this book to Terence, my son. At four, he is too young to understand the story of the Chinese in Canada. But in time he will have to learn the meaning of being a Chinese-Canadian. It is my hope that this book will inform him and future generations of Chinese-Canadians about their roots in this country.

Introduction

The 1981 Census of Canada reported roughly 290,000 Canadians of Chinese origin (Statistics Canada, 1981a, table 1); Chinese made up about 1 per cent of the population. About 75 per cent of them resided in British Columbia and Ontario, with Toronto and Vancouver accounting for 60 per cent of all Chinese in Canada (Statistics Canada, 1981b). Until 1981 this group of Canadians represented about half of one per cent or less of the country's population. Before 1901 the overwhelming majority of the Chinese in Canada resided in British Columbia; after that date they also settled in other provinces. By 1941 slightly more than half of the Chinese population in Canada lived in British Columbia, and 18 per cent in Ontario (Statistics Canada, 1941: vol. 1, tables 32–3).

Aside from the indigenous people, no other racial or ethnic group had experienced such harsh treatment in Canada as the Chinese. Anti-Chinese sentiments were high in British Columbia in the nineteenth century, and except for a few years after the arrival of the Chinese in British Columbia in 1858, the history of the province was marred by a long-lasting anti-Chinese movement. Anti-orientalism was common among politicians, union leaders, white workers, and employers, although each group benefited directly or indirectly from the presence of the Chinese. In this sense the Chinese in Canada, like those in the United States, were the 'indispensable enemy' (Saxton, 1971) of the state.

The same social and economic forces that had driven many European immigrants to North America earlier in the nineteenth century also drove many to emigrate from China to Canada and the U.S. during the latter half of the century. These waves of migration were propelled, on the one hand, by poverty at home and drawn, on the other, by opportunities abroad—a classic case of disparity between rich and poor nations. But unlike the European immigrants, who were generally accepted into Canadian society either as homesteaders on the prairies or as workers in the urban labour force, the Chinese were never considered a permanent feature of Canada. They were simply recruited as cheap labour to answer the shortage of white workers here.

It was no accident that the Dominion government of Canada

passed the first anti-Chinese bill in 1885, the same year the trans-continental Canadian Pacific Railway was completed. Earlier, the federal government had been so concerned about the shortage of labour in the west that it was unwilling to restrict Chinese immigration, despite requests from British Columbia. Between 1875 and 1923 British Columbia passed numerous bills to restrict the civil rights of the Chinese. Finally, in 1923, the federal government passed the Chinese Immigration Act, which excluded the Chinese from entering Canada for twenty-four years before it was repealed.

The Chinese gained the right to vote in the first few years after the Second World War. With the repeal of the Chinese Immigration Act in 1947, and subsequent changes in the Canadian immigration policy, they were allowed to immigrate on a limited basis. The volume of immigration was small in the two decades after the war, as Canada maintained its traditional policy of favouring immigrants from Europe and the United States over those from the Third World. But with the changes in immigration policy enacted in 1967 a larger volume of Chinese immigrants began to enter Canada. By 1981 over 60 per cent of the Chinese in Canada had immigrated after 1967 (Statistics Canada, 1981b).

The experiences of the Chinese in Canada may be grouped into three distinct periods. The exclusion era runs from 1923 to 1947, during which time no Chinese were allowed to immigrate to Canada and those already here were denied many of their civil rights. The period before the exclusion, between 1858 and 1923, witnessed the emergence of institutional racism, which made the Chinese in Canada frequent targets of racial antagonism and attacks. The end of the Second World War marked a new epoch as the Chinese gained their civil rights and began to build a new post-war community.

The development of the Chinese community in Canada was largely constrained by exogenous factors over which the Chinese had little control. By the turn of the century they had been virtually reduced to second-class citizens in Canada. Subjected to social, economic, and residential segregation in Canadian society, they responded by retreating into their own ethnic enclaves to avoid competition and hostility from white Canadians. Ironically, these unfavourable external conditions enabled ethnic businesses and associations to thrive in the Chinese community. Thus in many ways the emergence of these ethnic institutions had more to do with institutional racism in Canada than with a traditional culture purportedly transplanted from China.

The Chinese community in Canada before the war displayed several characteristics that were largely produced by government policies. Since the first Chinese in Canada were almost all men, the restriction on immigration after 1885 and the exclusion after 1923 resulted in a married-bachelor society. With few women, the growth of a second generation of Chinese-Canadians was greatly inhibited. Consequently the Chinese population in Canada shrank drastically from 1931 to 1951. It was not until after the war, when changes in the immigration policy enabled many Chinese to reunite with their families, that conjugal family life was gradually restored. In addition, the lines of work the Chinese could follow were limited.

Contemporary Chinese-Canadians are very different socially and occupationally from their ancestors who came in the last century. Immigrating in a different era, these new arrivals came from a more heterogeneous background. Many had professional and technical qualifications, and together with an emergent second generation of Chinese-Canadians they began to form a new middle class. At the same time, the large volume of post-war immigrants increased the foreign-born segment of the Chinese community. Consequently, despite its history of approximately 130 years in Canada, the Chinese community shows many linguistic and social features characteristic of first-generation immigrants. Notwithstanding their occupational and educational mobility, Chinese-Canadians today still experience racial discrimination in the Canadian labour market. They are also periodically reminded by various racial incidents that their origin remains a handicap in Canadian society.

Although this book focuses on the Chinese in Canada, it is in many ways a reflection of Canadian society and how it treats a racial minority. If in retrospect Canadians find it absurd to have imposed such extreme treatment on a racial minority that had made many contributions to the building of the west without posing any actual threat to Canadian society, they must find it equally difficult to accept either the internment of Japanese-Canadians during the Second World War or the continuing segregation of native people on reserves. These absurdities have occurred too frequently to be dismissed as historical accidents, and in the search for explanations it is often tempting to attribute them to the idiosyncracies of the groups being discriminated against. After all, the victims are visibly different from white Canadians. Thus the perception that the Chinese were physically different and the belief that they were culturally inferior made it possible for the average Canadian of the time to accept the injustices that were imposed on them. Thus too the behaviours, habits, and living conditions of the Chinese were used to show their unassimilable character and justify their mistreatment. The injustices done to racial minorities cannot be understood outside the context of social and economic developments in Canada and the structural contradictions that are inherent in such developments.

At the outset the Chinese could not be assimilated into Canadian society because they were never allowed to be assimilated. Their marginal position in Canadian society was a consequence of institutional racism, not of an alien culture. If the Chinese community appeared foreign to white Canadians, it was because its social isolation, vice activities, and poor living conditions ran counter to middle-class standards. These features were not products of a traditional culture: they were the results of racial oppression and societal alienation.

Throughout the history of the Chinese in Canada, their oppression and survival have had little directly to do with either their race or their culture. For example, just as there was no causal link between the skin colour of blacks and slavery,[1] the racial background of the Chinese cannot be held responsible for the menial jobs they had in the nineteenth century. Rather, the racial factor was conveniently used to justify unequal treatment once Canada had become dependent on the Chinese as a cheap source of labour. Likewise, the structure of the Chinese community in Canada had much less to do with the persistence of Confucian culture than with discriminatory Canadian policies. In the process of adapting to a hostile social environment the Chinese mobilized whatever resources were available to them, including elements that might otherwise have become dormant in their cultural repertoire, such as the remote kinship ties used in building ethnic businesses. If the Chinese culture played a part in their adaptation and survival in Canada, it was not a primordial culture that was at work. Instead, it was a new Chinese-Canadian culture that reflected both the experiences of the past and the challenges of the present. In this sense, the key to understanding the Chinese in Canada lies in the structure of Canadian society rather than in a traditional culture supposedly brought over from China.

Sociological themes of racial inequality

In their preoccupation with culture to explain the meaning of race, social scientists have often overlooked how societal barriers restrict the options and opportunities of racial minorities. For example, the classical approach to ethnic inequality tends to focus on cultural identities (Shibutani and Kwan, 1965), attitudinal profiles (Williams, 1964), and psychological characteristics (Rosen, 1956, 1959) as key ways of stratifying ethnic and racial groups. The theme of cultural deprivation and low economic achievement is echoed in many sociological writings. Rosen (1956, 1959), for example, argues that differential ethnic mobility in North America may be explained by ethnic variations on what he calls an 'achievement syndrome', that is, the psychological and cultural orientation toward achievement.[2] Hence groups such as Jews and white Protestants have a higher rate of upward mobility than Italians and blacks because they are more likely to hold achievement motivation, achievement values, and higher educational aspirations. Similarly, Lewis (1959, 1966a, 1966b) suggests that the under-achievement of many racial groups may be explained by what he sees as a 'culture of poverty'. In his own words, the culture of poverty 'has a structure, a rationale, and defense mechanisms without which the poor could hardly carry on' (Lewis, 1964: 150). He further argues that the poverty culture is a way of life that is passed on from generation to generation through the family. Lewis's description implies that the inability of some racial and ethnic groups to get rid of a handicapped culture explains why they are poor. Perhaps the clearest statement in this respect comes from Wagley and Harris (1959). In their book *Minorities in the New World* they argue that the adaptive capacity of a minority group determines its socio-economic status, and that such a capacity is dependent upon the group's cultural preparedness. Hence Jews and French-Canadians are economically more successful than native people and blacks because of their higher adaptability.

Critics of such cultural explanations (for example, Valentine [1968]) point out the ideological bias in blaming the victims for their misfortunes and the political implications in shifting attention from structural barriers that are distinctly apart from culture. Academically, cultural explanations are hard to defend when cultural values and achievement orientations often reflect more the consequences of social inequality than its causes.

More recently, the application of status-attainment models to racial and ethnic stratification (Duncan and Duncan, 1968; Featherman, 1971; Cuneo and Curtis, 1975; Boyd, et al., 1985) has gained popularity. Using the basic formulation of a career cycle (Blau and Duncan, 1967), status-attainment models treat racial and ethnic stratification as resulting from the differential marketable resources, such as skills and credentials, that individuals bring to the labour market. The findings from status-attainment models largely affirm the importance of structural variables, in particular those pertaining to prior ascribed and achieved statuses, and cast doubt on the relevance of psychological or motivation attributes to status differentiation. Despite the apparent success of these models, a substantial portion of inequality remains unexplained, leading some (Jencks, et al., 1972) to speculate on luck, and others (Light and Wong, 1975) to revert to a conjoint model of both cultural and institutional factors in accounting for inequality.[3]

The limitation of status-attainment models is partly methodological and partly theoretical. In most instances racial and ethnic stratification is measured along a status scale that frequently conceals the qualitative meaning, essential to class analysis,[4] of occupational categories. Moreover, the way most of these models are set up does not permit inquiry into the characteristics of the labour market beyond the level of individual attributes. In the hierarchy of statuses, individuals and social groups differ only in a matter of degree (Horan, 1978). Social categories based on relationships of production are ignored in the analysis. The world of status attainment is a neoclassical free market where individuals compete for social achievement. Consequently, alternative models of market structuration and productive relationships never have a chance of being considered in the framework of status attainment (Horan, 1978).

There is an obvious need to study the broader market features, beyond individual deficiencies, as a means of understanding how racial groups are incorporated into the capitalist economy. The challenge here is to be able to understand race not as a superficial physical or cultural trait, but as an objective reality that has a place in the process of capitalist production. Contrary to popular belief, racial groups are not primordial entities with uniform cultures. Nevertheless, superficial physical and cultural features are often used as social criteria, among others, to organize, process, and reward people in the capitalist market. In this way race provides a rational means of using what otherwise would be an irrational attribute to fractionalize social classes. Social fractions are created through job segregation, wage discrimination, and unequal treatments that extend from the job market to other spheres such as housing, education, and social services. On the ideological level, various forms of racism and ethnocentrism further divide social classes as they provide justifications for differential treatments. As society becomes so stratified along ethnic and racial grounds that good neighbourhoods, higher-paying jobs, and social influence become identifiable with race, it is inevitable that unequal social standings become associated with different origins. The low social status of racialized groups is in part defined by the low-paying jobs they hold, and in turn that social stigma further bars them from entering higher-paying positions. Consequently, in addition to the class conflicts typical of a capitalist system, there is a racial antagonism that is based in part on the attempts of higher-paying groups to protect their interests by preventing lower-paying groups from encroaching on their privileged positions (Bonacich, 1972, 1975, 1976), and in part on racist and ethnocentric ideologies that serve to justify their efforts. In this respect racial groups are exceptionally vulnerable to social stigmatization because of superficial physical differences and a low status that is largely determined by the colonial legacy.

In a racialized society, in which racial origin affects the prospects for employment, the disadvantaged groups are more compelled to seek lower-paying and less desirable jobs as discrimination makes higher-paying jobs less accessible to them. In other words, social fractionalization ensures a constant supply of cheap labour by classifying some racial groups as undesirable, thus making them less marketable for higher-paying positions and more available for lower-paying ones.

The theoretical approach that locates inequality in a larger societal context, beyond individual attributes and cultural idiosyncrasies, is not entirely novel. For example, Blauner's discussion of the 'internal colony' (1972), Bonacich's formulation of the 'split labour market' (1972, 1975), and Connelly's use of the 'reserve army of labour' (1976) are refreshing attempts to describe how the structuration of the capitalist economy sets the parameters of opportunities for social groups.

Ultimately, the success of a theoretical perspective depends on its heuristic value in explaining the empirical reality. The case of the Chinese offers academics an excellent opportunity to sharpen their theoretical tools in unravelling the maze of tangled historical and contemporary facts underlying the relations between the Chinese and their Canadian host society.

I

THE DEVELOPMENT OF
INSTITUTIONAL RACISM

1

Chinese Emigration

Chinese immigration to Canada began around 1858.[1] In response to the gold rush in the Fraser Valley, British Columbia, the Chinese initially migrated from the west coast of the United States, where many had been engaging in placer mining (Lamb, 1977). Subsequently, however, they came directly from China, especially between 1881 and 1885, when the Canadian Pacific Railway was constructed.

The available statistics indicate that the Chinese population in British Columbia grew slowly in the first two decades following their arrival and more rapidly thereafter. On January 26, 1860, the Victoria *Daily Colonist* mentioned 1,175 Chinese miners operating around the Fraser Valley. Between 1862 and 1864 there were a few thousand Chinese miners reported in the mining areas of British Columbia (Lee, 1967: 62). Between 1876 and 1880, the four years prior to the construction of the CPR, the number of Chinese arriving by ship in Canada was only 2,326. But the number rose to 2,939 in 1881, and 8,083 in 1882, before tapering off to 2,223 in 1884.[2] This wave of immigration substantially increased the Chinese population in Canada, which rose from 2,500 in 1860 (Woodsworth 1941: 20) to 4,383 in 1881 (Dept. of Agriculture, 1886: 48), and to 9,126 in 1891 (Dept. of Agriculture, 1893: 134).

In many ways the pattern of recruiting Chinese labourers to Canada was similar to Chinese recruitment to the United States, which began a decade earlier. With the discovery of gold in the Sacramento Valley, California, in 1848 came the demand for goods, provisions, and labour. Three Chinese pioneers were reported to have arrived in California in 1848. A year later there were 54 Chinese in California. By 1852 the number had increased to 11,787 (Bancroft, 1890: 336), and in 1860 the U.S. Census recorded 34,933 Chinese.[3] The Chinese were recruited largely as contract labour to work in mines and in similar labour-intensive jobs. The Pacific Mail Steamship Company and the Chinese Six Companies[4] cooperated in a scheme of coolie trade whereby both parties profited as middlemen in transporting and contracting Chinese labourers to American employers (Li, 1978). Between 1866 and 1869, when the Central Pacific Railroad was built, the railroad company contracted 10,000 Chinese to drill the Sierra tunnel and construct the line across the deserts of Nevada and Utah (Saxton, 1971: 4; U.S. Congress, Committee to Investigate Chinese Immigration, 1877: 15-16). While the Chinese were viewed as socially inferior, white miners and employers often accepted them as cheap labourers for performing menial work. This attitude was well summarized by one witness who appeared before a Congressional committee to investigate Chinese immigration in 1877:

> The Mongolian . . . ceased to be a curiosity in our midst, but to the contrary, was pronounced a blessing. He filled a vacuum. He came to labor, and found ready employment. The 'cute' Yankee was quick to discover that John Chinaman was a mere labor machine, and utilized him accordingly. (U.S. Congress, Committee to Investigate Chinese Immigration, 1877: 35)

As will be seen later, this utilitarian mentality regarding the Chinese was widely shared by industrialists and politicians in Canada. The Chinese were considered useful to the development of western Canada but were not desirable citizens. Historically, there was a striking similarity in the way the Chinese were treated in the United States and Canada. The resemblance had to do with the structural imperative of both countries to rely on a racialized labour force for capital accumulation, at a time when the shortage of white workers rendered industrial expansion difficult. The subsequent public outcry against oriental labour and the response of the state through policies of racism and exclusion reflected more the structural contradictions of capitalist expansion than a mere psychological phobia on the part of white Americans or Canadians towards people of a different race.

Conditions in China

Although the discovery of gold and the construction of railroads were the immediate events triggering the immigration of Chinese to Canada, it is in a larger historical context that this process of labour exodus may be best explained. As in other international migrations, it was a combination of factors in the home country and the receiving state, which served as 'pushing' and 'pulling' forces, that propelled the wave of human movement from one country to another.

Up until the middle of the nineteenth century China was an autonomous state that had been under the imperial rule of the Ch'ing dynasty since 1644. The year 1838 marked the beginning of foreign domination of China, when she fought unsuccessfully against Britain in the Opium War (1839–42). The defeat led to the signing of the Treaty of Nanjing (Nanking), by which Britain obtained certain trading and territorial rights from China. Britain's victory was followed by many other foreign invasions, each one resulting in an unequal treaty that infringed upon the territorial and economic integrity of China. Between 1838 and 1900 Britain, France, Germany, Austria, Japan, the United States, Italy, and Russia engaged in a series of wars with China in her territories and succeeded in securing trading and other rights from the Chinese government (Wakeman, 1975; Hsu, 1970).

From the early part of the nineteenth century the imperial rule of China had begun to show signs of internal weakness. Rapid population growth in the eighteenth century, for example, was not followed by a corresponding increase in farm yields, nor by new economic opportunities (Ho, 1967; Perkins, 1969). According to one estimate China's population almost doubled, from somewhere between 200 and 250 million in 1750 to about 410 million in 1850, while cultivated land increased only from 950 million *mu* (*mou*)[5] in 1766 to 1,210 million *mu* in 1873 (Perkins, 1969: 216, 240). Towards the second half of the nineteenth century China also suffered from declining productivity in farm yields and frequent natural disasters such as floods and famines. These social and natural calamities further intensified the social contradiction in China, characterized by the control of absentee landlords and the poverty of peasant-tenants.[6]

By the same period the industrial revolution in Europe, and later America, had completely transformed many traditional agricultural societies into industrial nations. Great Britain, France, and other western countries became the core of the capitalist world system that had been emerging since the sixteenth century (Wallerstein, 1979). By the nineteenth century these countries were seeking international hinterlands for exporting their finished products and for extracting raw materials and cheap labour to be used for further capitalist production. China became attractive to these capitalist countries as a weak nation with a large potential market. The western powers were so determined to expand their trade with the Orient that, despite competition among themselves, they joined forces on many occasions in forcibly imposing unequal trading treaties on China. Their preoccupation with the Chinese market also led to many attempts to shorten the sea routes to China, including the building of the Suez Canal in 1859 (Woodsworth, 1941: 7–18).

The penetration of foreign capitalism into China accelerated the breakdown of the Chinese economy. This social process was analyzed by Mao (1967) as follows:

> Foreign capitalism played an important part in the disintegration of China's social economy; on the one hand, it undermined the foundations of her self-sufficient natural economy and wrecked the handicraft industries both in the cities and in the peasants' homes, and on the other, it hastened the growth of a commodity economy in town and country. . . . The destruction of the natural economy created a commodity market for capitalism, while the bankruptcy of large numbers of peasants and handicraftsmen provided it with a labour market. (Mao, 1967: 309–10)

The social contradictions in China were intensified after the Opium War. A combination of social and economic factors eventually led to the Taiping Rebellion, a peasant revolt that lasted fourteen years, from 1850 to 1864 (Shurmann and Schell, 1967). Both the duration and the extent of the rebellion clearly reflected the desperation of starving peasants and the frustration of intellectuals in trying to improve adverse social and economic conditions through extreme measures.

Despite an imperial edict that imposed a stiff penalty on those leaving the empire of China without a special permit[7] (Morse, 1918: 163–5), many in the provinces of Guangdong (Kwangtung) and Fujian (Fukien) ventured abroad to seek a better living. The proximity of these two provinces to the sea probably made it easier for peasants there to emigrate. But poor economic conditions and the unstable political climate were the major reasons why so many left their home country even for a laborious livelihood overseas. Many Chinese immigrants to Canada came from a limited number of counties near the city of Canton (Lai, 1975), among them the county of Taishan (T'ai-shan, known as Sanning before 1911).[8] Lai (1975) estimates that about 23 per cent of the Chinese in British Columbia around 1884–85 were from Tais-han, and between 1885 and 1903 as many as 45 per cent of the Chinese entering Canada came from that county, based on a random sample of Chinese recorded in the official General Reg-isters of Chinese Immigration to Canada.[9] The county of Taishan was hardest hit with natural disasters in the latter half of the nineteenth century; between 1851 and 1908 it suffered fourteen major floods, seven typhoons, four earthquakes, two droughts, four plagues, and five famines (Liu, Hirata, and Zheng 1980: 26). In addition, a local war between clans, from 1856 to 1864, was directly responsible for the deaths of twenty to thirty thousand people (Liu, Hirata, and Zheng, 1980). Pushing many peasants to the brink of starvation, these natural and social calamities made them vulnerable to recruitment for the overseas labour market.

Mechanisms of Chinese immigration

Starting in the middle of the nineteenth century, large waves of Chinese emigrants were recruited to Southeast Asia, the Pacific Islands, Australia, and America to work on plantations and in mines (Campbell, 1969; Stewart, 1970). The Chinese who came to Canada represented only a portion of those who went overseas.

With the decline of the slave trade the plantations in Southeast Asia and Latin America were in great need of cheap labour. The slavery system that had been central to the plantation economy became inefficient as capitalism transformed many individual farms into corporate enterprises. At the same time, industrial expansion created increasing demands on free labour both as workers and as consumers. By the middle of the nineteenth century in America, for example, the concentration of landhold-ing and slaveholding prohibited both further development of industrial production and the corresponding expansion of the capitalist market. (In many ways, the American Civil War can be seen as an attempt to resolve the contradiction between the industrializing North and the slave-dependent South with respect to use of labour and land [Genovese, 1967; Greene, 1971].) It was against this historical background that coolie[10] trade burgeoned in the middle of the nineteenth century.

In many cases the Chinese emigration was not totally volun-

tary. Many European ships, with the assistance of Chinese com-
pradores, engaged in a scheme of coolie trade that involved
shipping large numbers of indentured Chinese from southeastern China to America, the West Indies, and certain South Pacific
islands (Morse, 1918; Campbell, 1969; Stewart, 1970). Hong
Kong and Macao became the centres of the coolie trade (MacNair,
1927: 409–18; Irick, 1982); between 1845 and 1873 the number of
Chinese contract labourers recruited overseas is estimated to be
322,593, of whom 89 per cent were shipped from those two cities
(Chen, 1981: 541–2). Although there is no evidence to suggest
that the Chinese who came to North America were brought in
as slaves, many were recruited as indentured labourers (Campbell, 1969). A commercial company would advance the passage
ticket and a small sum of money to the Chinese, who in return
would accept employment arranged by the company, with a
portion of their monthly wage being deducted to repay the cred-
itor. As a certain Dr. McInnis, a member of Parliament from
British Columbia, explained the arrangement to the 1885 Royal
Commission on Chinese Immigration:

> They [the Chinese] give bonds, before leaving China, to Chinese
> companies to work for them for a term of five or ten years, and
> all that the Company have to do in order to carry out their part of
> the contract is to furnish them with the bare necessities of life and
> their clothing, and the Company have all their earnings. After
> they serve their time, of course, they go then and work for them-
> selves. (Royal Commission, 1885: xxv)

This system of contract labour was also used widely in the
United States to procure Chinese workers. The practice was dis-
cussed by various witnesses at the California State Senate hearing in 1876 (Senate of California, 1876). Similar testimonies were
recorded in the report of a U.S. Congressional committee to
investigate Chinese immigration a year later (U.S. Congress,
1877). A San Francisco shoe manufacturer gave the following
testimony at the California hearing:

> We contracted for them [Chinese], for two years, with Yuchuy-
> lung Company. We made contracts with them to furnish us so
> many men for a certain price, and we paid the money to that
> company. They furnish us as many men as we want, and we have
> nothing to do with the Chinamen, except to work them. . . . We
> hold back from each man's wages a certain amount to secure

fulfillment of their contract. Our contract provides that when a
man goes away the company shall furnish us another. . . . When
they violate the contract, we appropriate this deduction which we
have made from their wages. (Senate of California, Committee on
Chinese Immigration, 1876: 50)

It is difficult to estimate how many Chinese were recruited to
Canada as indentured labourers. Many of those who immigrated
during the mining period of the 1860s and 1870s no doubt came
as independent miners and labourers. Of the 15,701 Chinese
estimated to have entered Canada between 1881 and 1884 (Campbell, 1969: 37) about 6,500 were employed directly by contractors
building the western section of the Canadian Pacific Railway
(Lee, 1967: 128; Campbell, 1969: 37). The initial crew of Chinese
railroad workers was recruited by Andrew Onderdonk, the con-
tractor for building the section in British Columbia. In 1880
Onderdonk asked Lian Chang Company, a Chinese firm organized by Li Tian Pei, a Chinese merchant in the United States,
to recruit 1,500 Chinese workers from the Portland area. The next
year Onderdonk brought in 2,000 Chinese from Hong Kong
through the same company (Lee, 1967: 126-8). Two other
Chinese firms, Tai Chong and Lee Chuck, were involved in contracting Chinese workers from Hong Kong in 1882, and two
transportation companies, Stahlschmidt and Ward, and Welch
and Rithet, were engaged in shipping them; of the 8,000 Chinese
landing in Victoria in 1882, over 5,000 were transported by
Stahlschmidt and Ward (Con, et al., 1982: 21).

The exact terms under which these Chinese workers were
recruited are unclear. It is likely that the recruiting company
would advance some money to the Chinese workers, arrange
their employment in work teams under the supervision of over-
seers, and collect the money back from their monthly pay in
Canada. The workers travelled in organized groups to railroad
camps where an agent of the contracting firm would reside.
These Chinese labour camps were set up at Yale, Port Moody,
and Savona's Ferry, with as many as 1,000 workers in each one
(Con, et al., 1982: 22). There is evidence to suggest that after
working for the railroad company for a few years the Chinese
workers remained destitute. On November 21, 1885, the Executive Council of British Columbia sent a report to the Secretary of
State in Ottawa describing the poor conditions of many Chinese

discharged by the railroad company at the completion of the CPR. The report suggests that the Chinese coolies were working under an indenture system of sorts:

> Thousands of these people, having been summarily discharged by the railway contractors, and their earnings having been absorbed by their rapacious masters or owners, are now left in a starving condition, and unless substantial relief be extended to them there is every prospect of their perishing during the winter. (Public Archives of Canada, 1886)

Many of these displaced railroad workers took up casual employment in the logging, mining, farming, and canning industries of British Columbia (Lai, 1973). But the harsh economic conditions continued for at least two decades after the completion of the railway, becoming so desperate that between 1890 and 1914 the Chinese Consolidated Benevolent Association in Victoria made three attempts to discourage further immigration from China (Lai, 1973).

Towards the turn of the century another form of contract labour was popular among a number of industries in British Columbia. This system involved white employers contracting with Chinese recruiters to supply them with Chinese work gangs. The Chinese contractors in turn advanced the Chinese workers wages that were later recuperated from white employers. The canneries in British Columbia employed about 6,000 Chinese in 1901 using this system (Ward, 1978: 17). This pattern was confirmed by a witness who testified before the 1907 Royal Commission investigating the losses sustained by the Chinese and Japanese during a race riot in Vancouver (Royal Commission, 1907). The witness admitted that, representing a firm of Chinese merchants, he had a contract with a canning company to supply it with with 80 to 100 Chinese men every year, paying them not less than $65 a month. He in return was to receive a certain sum for each case packed in the canning company (Sessional Paper, 1909: 105).

It is incorrect to assume that all Chinese came to Canada as contract labourers. Some were independent miners, merchants, domestic servants, and other service workers employed in various industries. But whether they came as contract or as independent workers, most were engaged in menial work for which employers had difficulty finding white labourers. The scanty evidence on the employment pattern of the Chinese clearly shows their marginal occupational positions in 1885. Among the

10,000 Chinese in British Columbia in 1885 were 2,900 railroad workers, 1,468 miners, 1,612 farm labourers, 700 food canners, and 708 lumber workers. Store owners and merchants accounted for only 121 of the Chinese at that time (Royal Commission, 1885: 363–5).

The social background of Chinese emigrants

Most Chinese who came to Canada in the nineteenth century originated from a limited number of rural counties in southern China. For example, Lai (1975) found that of the 5,056 Chinese in British Columbia in the early 1880s who made donations to the Chinese Consolidated Benevolent Association in Victoria, 64 per cent originated from the four counties of Taishan (T'ai-shan), Kaiping (K'ai-p'ing), Xinhui (Hsin-hui), and Enping (En-p'ing); Taishan alone was the home county for 23 per cent.

With the exception of a small number of merchants, the majority of Chinese emigrants came from the lower stratum of Chinese society. The records of the Chinese entering Canada around the turn of the century provide a glimpse of the occupational background of these early immigrants. Table 1.1 shows the stated occupation of 4,564 Chinese who entered Canada between 1885 and 1903. The data indicate that 72.5 percent were labourers; merchants and storekeepers accounted for only 5.7 per cent. Among the 4,638 Chinese only 50 were women, 30 of whom were wives. In a study of Chinese who came to Canada between 1910 and 1923, Li (1982) found that many immigrated at an early age and had little or no working experience prior to immigration, aside from working in agricultural fields. Most had limited formal schooling and spoke practically no English before coming to Canada. Like many of their predecessors who went overseas, the Chinese who came in the early part of the twentieth century left home to escape economic hardship in the search for better employment opportunities. In many cases they borrowed from relatives to finance the trip and paid back the loans when they had had a chance to work and save up in Canada. As one immigrant described it:

> We were poor and starving, and we needed money at home. We had to borrow money to come over here, and when we came over here, we had to work hard to pay back the money that we owed. (Interview transcripts, cited in Li, 1982: 532)

TABLE 1.1

STATED OCCUPATION OF A RANDOM SAMPLE OF CHINESE
ENTERING CANADA, 1885–1903

Occupation	Number	%
Cook	136	3.0
Farmer	309	6.8
Labourer	3308	72.5
Laundryman	267	5.9
Merchant	232	5.1
Miner	44	1.0
Storekeeper	28	0.6
Student	21	0.5
Wife	30	0.7
Other	189	4.1
Total	4564	100.2

SOURCE: Calculations based on a 10% random sample selected from all Chinese recorded in the *General Registers of Chinese Immigration*, 1885–1903 (Public Archives of Canada, RG 76, vols. 694–703).

The mobility dream and sojourner orientation

Like many European immigrants who came to North America early in the nineteenth century, the Chinese migrated with the hope of making a fortune in the new world. But unlike most Europeans, who were accepted as permanent immigrants, the Chinese were viewed by white settlers and employers as aliens who could be utilized in lower-paying jobs but were not to be trusted as social equals. Anti-orientalism was strong among white British Columbians, despite the indispensable contribution made by the Chinese in developing the pioneer industries in the province. Virtually every conceivable social evil was blamed on the them, including epidemics, overcrowding, prostitution, opium-smoking, and corruption (Ward, 1978: 3–22). Many allegations were based on stereotypes of China, and the Chinese character was believed to have come from a debased civilization (Ward, 1978). The Chinese were also blamed by the labouring class for depressing wages, since they were generally paid less than white workers and at times were used as scabs in labour disputes. At the hearings of the 1885 Royal Commission the Chinese were often described as useful to the development of pioneer industries when the labour supply was short; but as soon as white labourers became more available they were viewed as taking away opportunities defined as belonging to white people (Li, 1979a).

Among the many assaults on the Chinese culture and character were accusations that the Chinese were unassimilable and that they only took savings out of the country with no plan of settling in Canada (Royal Commission, 1885). While in fact many Chinese stayed in Canada permanently, most did emigrate with the dream of returning to China rich; their hope of success was to work hard in Canada so that one day they could retire in their homeland. Meanwhile they aspired to visit China periodically, where they could unite with their family for a short period of time (Li, 1982). Although it was exaggerated, there was some truth to the following description of the Chinese emigrating during the latter half of the nineteenth century:

> Generally speaking, no Chinese will leave his home to seek a fortune at a distance unless he is in some way driven to do so. . . . No Chinese leaves his home not intending to return. His hope is always to come back rich, to die and be buried where his ancestors are buried. (Cited in Purcell, 1966: 30)

This aspiration is sometimes described by sociologists (Siu, 1953) as a 'sojourner orientation', a transient mentality that prevents immigrants from making long-term commitments to the host society. The mobility dream was not unique among the Chinese, however, as the emotional tie to the homeland and the desire to retire comfortably must have been familiar to many European immigrants crossing the Atlantic in the eighteenth and nineteenth centuries.

There is little evidence to indicate that many Chinese emigrants were able to realize their mobility dream of retiring rich in their homeland. There is also little to support the suggestion that the 'sojourner orientation' prevented overseas Chinese from establishing family roots in the receiving society. Most Chinese who went overseas ended up settling in the host country. In Southeast Asia, where hostility towards the Chinese was more subtle than in North America, the Chinese developed an elaborate community structure, typical of permanent settlers, shortly after their initial arrival. The emergence and persistence of Chinese communities in Thailand (Skinner, 1957), Indonesia (Willmott, 1960), the Philippines (Wickberg, 1965), Cambodia (Willmott, 1967), Vietnam, and Malaysia (Purcell, 1966) suggest that whatever transient mentality Chinese immigrants might have had did not seem to affect their ability to establish permanent networks in the host societies. This point was succinctly argued by Huang Tsun Hsien in his testimony before the 1885 Royal Commission:

> I would like to say this. That it is charged the Chinese do not emigrate to foreign countries to remain, but only to earn a sum of money and return to their homes in China. It is only about thirty years since our people commenced emigrating to other lands. A large number have gone to the Straits Settlements, Manilla, Cochin-China and the West India Islands, and are permanently settled there with their families. In Cuba, fully seventy-five per cent have married native women, and adopted those Islands as their future homes. Many of those living in the Sandwich Islands have done the same. This, of course, depends wholly upon their treatment in any country they emigrate to. . . . You must recollect that the Chinese immigrants coming to this country are denied all the rights and privileges extended to others in the way of citizenship; the laws compel them to remain aliens. I know a great many Chinese will be glad to remain here permanently with their families, if they are allowed to be naturalized and can enjoy privileges and rights. (Royal Commission, 1885: xi-xii)

As will be seen later, it was largely structural forces, not subjective predispositions, that compelled the Chinese to remain marginal in Canadian society. The Chinese were subjected to numerous legislative controls and forms of discrimination that few other immigrant groups in Canada experienced.

2

Racism Against the Chinese

In the initial period of their arrival in British Columbia the Chinese were not treated with overt hostility, although there were subdued sentiments against them. Early newspaper reports were generally favourable; for example, a reporter for the London *Times* wrote in 1860 that there were 'no distinctions made against them [Chinese] in these colonies. . . . The great bulk of the population is very glad to see them coming into the country' (quoted in Woodsworth, 1941: 20). An article in the Victoria *British Colonist* in 1861 recognized the industriousness of the Chinese and their potential usefulness to Canada:

> We have plenty of room for many thousands of Chinamen. And notwithstanding they may not bring their wives with them to settle permanently in the country, nor build school-houses, churches, or acquire our language, but continue to live and work among themselves, yet there can be no shadow of a doubt but their industry enables them to add very largely to our own revenues and our circulating medium. (*British Colonist*, July 6, 1861, cited in Woodsworth, 1941: 21)

Between 1858 and 1868 both the *British Colonist* and the *Victoria Gazette* periodically carried news about the Chinese on the west coast. Although descriptions of Chinese were stereotypical, the tone tended to be humorous and not derogatory (Morton, 1974). Anti-Chinese sentiments in California, for instance, did not win much support in these two newspapers during this period (Morton, 1974).

Agitation against the Chinese began to grow when British Columbia experienced economic hardships. By 1866 good claims in placer mining were difficult to find, and the Chinese were frequently perceived as competitors who were willing to undercut white miners' wages (Woodsworth, 1941). In 1875, four years after British Columbia joined Confederation, it passed legislative bills to disenfranchise the Chinese (Kung, 1961–62), and in 1876 to prohibit hiring them in government projects (Woodsworth,

1941). When the Canadian Pacific Railway was completed in 1885 the federal government moved to restrict the immigration of Chinese to Canada (Li, 1979a).

Chinese labour and the opening of the west

From the outset the real Chinese question in Canada, as in the U.S. (Li, 1976), was in essence a question of how to exploit a cheap source of labour when the supply of white workers fell short of the increasing demands from the expanding industries of the west. The shortage of white labourers was created by a number of factors. During the 1860s and 1870s British Columbia was experiencing a long period of depression (Campbell, 1969), in part because many European miners were leaving Canada as the mine yields declined. For every census period after 1851–61 the volume of out-migration from Canada exceeded that of in-migration (Timlin, 1960). The existence of legal barriers to immigration in many European countries during this period also tended to deter large waves of immigrants from Europe (Timlin, 1960). Before the completion of the CPR the journey from east coast to west was both difficult and costly, and Europeans who made the trip through the United States usually ended up staying there (Campbell, 1969). By the time the CPR was to be constructed and new industries subsequently began to boom, white labourers were hard to obtain. The Chinese became attractive to many employers because of their large supply and cheaper cost.

There is little doubt, from the evidence presented before the 1885 commission, that Chinese labour was indispensable to the economic development of British Columbia. As Sir Matthew Begbie, Chief Justice of British Columbia, put it:

> I do not see how people would get on here at all without China-men. They do, and do well, what white women cannot do, and do what white men will not do. (Royal Commission, 1885: 75)

With respect to the achievements of the Chinese in various industries of British Columbia, Begbie summarized as follows:

> But as to the past, the undoubted facts are: 1st. That Chinamen are very largely, and till within a year, mainly, employed in all the labourious parts of our coal mines; 2nd. They constitute three-fourths of the working hands about every salmon cannery; 3rd. They are a very large majority of the labourers employed in gold mines; 4th. They are the model market gardeners of the province,

and produce the greater part of the vegetables grown here; 5th. They have been found to be absolutely indispensable in the construction of the railway; 6th. They are largely, sometimes, exclusively, employed in nearly every manufactory or undertaking of any description, not being under the authority of a board or council elected exclusively by white voters. (Ibid.)

During the hearings of the Commission the Chinese were commonly equated with no more than a piece of machinery or a horse, something with a use-value, to be maintained when other labour power was not available. For example, a merchant named Ward, engaged in a number of enterprises, testified as follows:

> It would be difficult to say what proportion (if any) Chinese immigration should bear to the immigration of white people, in order to advance the best interests of the colony and provide comfort of the people now here. This depends upon the amount of cheap white labour likely to be procurable. (Ibid.: 85)

The same mentality prevailed in the Royal Commission on Chinese and Japanese Immigration of 1902. Each chapter of the 1902 commission report dealt with one industry to examine the extent to which that industry had depended on Chinese labour, and whether further restriction on Chinese immigration might jeopardize its future development. The commissioners were forthright in raising the following question: 'Will the prohibition of further immigration of Chinese labour injuriously affect the various industries of the country?' (Royal Commission, 1902: 272). Both commissions came to the same basic conclusions with regard to the Chinese. They were perceived as undesirable and non-assimilable immigrants because of many alleged cultural and social peculiarities. Their labour, however, had been needed in mining, forestry, railroad construction, canning, and other industries where white workers were not available. The subsequent presence of large numbers of Chinese in Canada and the availability of more white labourers greatly reduced the need to import more Chinese. Therefore both commissions recommended restriction, in the form of a head tax, to control further Chinese immigration to Canada. The 1902 commission in particular was explicit about its view of the Chinese as a source of cheap labour and nothing else. The commissioners concluded that

> this class of immigration [Chinese] falls far short of that standard

so essential to the well-being of the country. From a Canadian
standpoint it is injurious, and in the interest of the nation any
further immigration ought to be prohibited. The great industries
will not suffer. There is a surplus of this class of labour at the
present time ready to enter any avenue of unskilled labour that
may open. (Royal Commission, 1902: 278)

The employment pattern of the Chinese in their first fifty years
in Canada shows how they answered the labour needs of British
Columbia. They were recruited for various labour-intensive
industries such as mining, railroad construction, land clearing,
public works, gardening, lumbering, salmon canning, and
domestic service (Royal Commission, 1902). With the exception
of domestic servants, the Chinese in each industry had similar
experiences. They were welcome as cheap labourers in a pioneer
industry where other labour was not readily available. Their participation, however, remained precarious. As long as they
accepted their menial position and avoided competition with
white workers they were tolerated in times of need. But as the
industries expanded and white workers became attracted to
them, employers began paying Chinese less than white workers.
Consequently the Chinese were perceived by white workers as
undercutting wages and weakening working-class solidarity.
White workers in each industry then began demanding the exclusion of Chinese. Agitation against the Chinese usually increased
during recessions, when they were particularly blamed for economic and social woes. This pattern of employment was well
summarized by Superintendent Robins of the Vancouver Coal
Mining and Land Company:

When the Chinese first came to this province they no doubt supplied a want then felt, and there [their] coming was encouraged
and welcomed, especially I may add by the Vancouver Coal Mining and Land Company [Limited], which I represent; but the
labouring population were always strongly averse to their introduction. At the time of their coming here my company had been
suffering from a strike of the white laborers, and we accepted the
Chinese as a weapon with which to settle the dispute. . . . White
people can now find remunerative employment. In fact, wages
are high enough to attract the best class of white labor. . . . The
encouragement given to the Chinese by employers of labor has
not been withdrawn up to the present time, whilst the anti-

Chinese feeling seems to have grown stronger every year. (Royal
Commission, 1885: xvi)

Anti-orientalism and legislative control

Few minority groups in Canada attracted so much public reaction
as the Chinese, and no other immigrant group was subjected to
the same legislative controls. Anti-orientalism was exceptionally
strong in British Columbia. Before the enactment of the Chinese
Immigration Act of 1885 there had already been many attempts
by British Columbia politicians to press the Dominion government to act on what was defined as the public menace. In 1879
a petition from Noah Shakespeare and 1,500 British Columbia
workers was presented to the Dominion House of Commons by
Amor de Cosmos, requesting the exclusion of Chinese from work
on the CPR. As a result a special committee was appointed to
investigate the matter (Campbell, 1969: 38–9). In 1882 the British
Columbia legislature demanded that the Dominion government
require CPR contractors to hire white workers and not Chinese,
but the request was rejected on the grounds that the government
had no means to restrict contractors (Munro, 1971: 43; Woodsworth, 1941: 29).

As early as 1875 the parliament of British Columbia had passed
a bill to disenfranchise the Chinese (Statutes of B.C. 1875, no.
2), and subsequent legislation continued to bar them from voting
in provincial (Statutes of B.C. 1895, c. 20; Statutes of B.C 1920,
c. 27) and municipal elections (Statutes of B.C. 1896, c. 38). Previously, in 1872 and 1874, there were unsuccessful attempts to
levy a special annual tax on the Chinese, on the grounds that
they were displacing white miners in coal fields (Woodsworth,
1941: 24–5). In 1878 there was another attempt to tax the Chinese
$40 a year, but the act was declared unconstitutional by the
Supreme Court of British Columbia (Woodsworth, 1941: 26). The
province of British Columbia passed bills in 1884 (Statutes of B.C.
1884, c. 3) and 1885 (Statutes of B.C. 1885, c. 13) to prevent the
immigration of Chinese by fining any who attempted entry into
the province and by punishing those assisting them. But both
bills were disallowed on the grounds that only the Dominion
government had the right to pass laws dealing with immigration.
Between 1884 and 1923 the British Columbia legislature suc-

cessfully passed numerous bills restricting the political and social rights of the Chinese. For example, a bill in 1884 disallowed Chinese from acquiring Crown lands and diverting water from natural channels (Statutes of B.C. 1884, c. 2). The Coal Mines Regulation Amendment Act of 1890 prevented them from working underground (Statutes of B.C. 1890, c. 33), and an amendment in 1903 prevented them from performing skilled jobs in coal mines (Statutes of B.C. 1903, c. 17). The Provincial Home Act of 1893 excluded Chinese from admission to the provincially established home for the aged and infirm (Statutes of B.C. 1893, c. 35); they were prohibited from being hired on public works in 1897 (Statutes of B.C. 1897, c. 1); and the Liquor License Act of 1899 stipulated that they were not entitled to hold a liquor license (Statutes of B.C. 1899, c. 39). Since their names were excluded from the provincial voters' list, Chinese were also barred from obtaining a hand-logger's license (Statues of B.C. 1903, c. 17). Because the provincial voters' list was used as a qualification, Chinese were also excluded from nomination for municipal office, school trustees, jury service, and election to the provincial legislature (Angus, 1937: 81). One of the conditions in sales of Crown timber was that Asiatics not be employed (Angus, 1937: 82). The Chinese were also barred from the professions of law and pharmacy (Angus, 1937: 83). The 1920 Provincial Elections Act reaffirmed that all Chinese were disqualified from voting (Statutes of B.C. 1920, c. 27).

Although some laws were not explicitly directed against any particular racial group, they implied a *de facto* discrimination against the Chinese. The Factories Act of 1922 forbade night employment in laundries and restricted the hours of operation from 7 A.M. to 7 P.M., excluding Sundays and holidays (Statutes of B.C. 1922, c. 25); since Chinese hand laundries operated long into the night, they were most affected by the law. The Civil Service Act of 1917 stipulated that no one could work in the civil service who was not a British subject (Statutes of B.C. 1917, c. 9). The Women's and Girls' Protection Act of 1923 specified that no one should employ a white or Indian woman or girl in places where morals might be in question (Statutes of B.C. 1923, c. 76). It was left up to the power of provincial or municipal police to prevent such employment in Chinese businesses.

British Columbia was not the only province that passed legislation against the Chinese. In Saskatchewan the Chinese were disenfranchised in 1908 (Statutes of Saskatchewan 1908, c. 2), and in 1912 the provincial legislature passed an act disallowing the employment of white females in restaurants and other businesses kept or managed by the Chinese (Statutes of Saskatchewan 1912, c. 17). The bill prompted the governments of Ontario and British Columbia to pass similar legislation in 1914 and 1923 respectively (Statutes of Ontario 1914, c. 40; Statutes of B.C. 1923, c. 76).

In addition to the many legislative exclusions of Chinese there were other attempts to reduce the competition from oriental labour. The British Columbia Fisheries Commission of 1922 recommended eliminating oriental fishermen from the fishing industry by reducing the number of licenses issued. As noted in the Commission's report, the question was

> not whether Oriental licenses should be reduced in number, but what percentage of reduction should be decided upon in order to bring about the displacement of orientals by white fishermen in the shortest possible time without disrupting the industry. (British Columbia Fisheries Commission, 1922: 11)

By 1885 British Columbia politicians were putting increasing pressure on the Dominion government to restrict Chinese immigration. Earlier the federal government had resisted any restriction for fear that a labour shortage might jeopardize the completion of the CPR. Prime Minister Macdonald was echoing such concerns when he frankly told the House of Commons in 1883:

> It will be all very well to exclude Chinese labour, when we can replace it with white labour, but until that is done, it is better to have Chinese labour than no labour at all. (Canada House of Commons Debates, 1883: 905)

This argument explains why the Prime Minister was reluctant to entertain an anti-Chinese bill before the CPR was completed. In restrospect it also becomes evident that legislative controls on the Chinese were inevitable, as soon as major projects of development were completed in British Columbia and Chinese labour became dispensable.

The first federal anti-Chinese bill was passed in 1885 when the CPR was completed. It took the form of a head tax of $50 imposed, with few exceptions, upon every person of Chinese origin entering the country (Statutes of Canada 1885, c. 71).[1] The same act stipulated that vessels to Canada could not carry more than one Chinese for every fifty tons of tonnage. Chinese entering Canada were then given a certificate of entry or residence, which had to be returned to the controller in exchange for a certificate of leave when they left Canada, even temporarily; otherwise they would not be allowed to return. In 1900 the head tax was raised to $100 (Statutes of Canada 1900, c. 32) and in 1903 to $500 (Statutes of Canada, 1903, c. 8). In addition to these immigration acts, the War-Time Elections Act (Statutes of Canada 1917, c. 39) stipulated that only those who qualified for provincial franchise could vote in federal elections. Since the Chinese were excluded from provincial elections in a number of provinces, including British Columbia and Saskatchewan, in these provinces they were in effect also disenfranchised in federal elections. Both the Dominion Elections Act of 1920 (Statutes of Canada 1920, c. 46) and its 1929 amendments (Statutes of Canada, 1929, c. 40) further stipulated that in addition to having provincial voting rights, all voters must be British subjects. These conditions virtually prevented Chinese from voting in federal elections.

But if the Chinese were denied basic citizenship rights, they were not immune from citizenship obligations. Woodsworth (1941: 142–3) noted that neither the income-tax act nor the taxation act provided any concessions for Chinese-Canadians, and the Dominion Militia Act did not exempt those not entitled to vote from conscription.

In 1923 the Canadian Parliament passed the Chinese Immigration Act, the most comprehensive act to exclude Chinese from entering the country and to control those already here (Statutes of Canada 1923, c. 38). According to the act, the entry to Canada of 'persons of Chinese origin or descent irrespective of allegiance or citizenship' would be restricted to diplomatic corps, children born in Canada to parents of Chinese race or descent, merchants, and students (Statutes of Canada 1923, c. 38, s. 5). All other Chinese were in essence excluded from entry. Those seeking admission were to be segregated from the public for examination. Section 10.2 of the Act stated:

> The examination of persons of Chinese origin or descent applying for admission or entry to Canada shall be separated and apart from the public and in the presence of such persons only as the Controller shall permit. (Statutes of Canada 1923, c. 38, s. 10)

The Chinese Immigration Act of 1923 also stipulated that every person of Chinese origin in Canada, irrespective of citizenship, was required to register with the government of Canada within twelve months after the act came into force and to obtain a certificate of such registration. Any Chinese who failed to register would be liable to a fine of up to $500 or imprisonment for up to twelve months, or both. Furthermore, every Chinese in Canada who intended to leave the country temporarily and return at a later date had to give written notice to the Controller before departure, specifying the foreign port or place he planned to visit and the route he intended to take. Those who had so registered before leaving Canada would be allowed to return within two years. Chinese leaving Canada without registering would be treated as new immigrants seeking entry upon their return. Even prior to the 1923 Act, the Department of Immigration and Colonization had been setting up regulations that restricted the admission of Chinese to limited categories. The Act virtually stopped any future immigration of Chinese to Canada, and legalized the inferior status of those already in the country. It was not until after the Second World War, in 1947, that the Chinese Immigration Act was repealed (Statutes of Canada 1947, c. 19).

Although the Chinese were not legally barred from becoming naturalized citizens of Canada, naturalization was difficult after 1923 (Angus, 1937: 86). Between 1915 and 1930, for example, only 349 Chinese were naturalized, and after 1931 an order-in-council required that those applying for Canadian citizenship obtain consent from the Ministry of the Interior in China (Privy Council 1931–1378).[2] Since the 1914 Naturalization Act also stated that wives took on the status of their husbands, a Chinese woman with Canadian citizenship automatically became an alien by marrying an alien Chinese (Statutes of Canada 1914, c. 44).[3]

Aside from numerous legislative controls, the Chinese were subjected to frequent racial hostilities and attacks. Among the most serious of these were the riots of 1887 and 1907 in Vancouver. Both were actions of wanton crowds aimed at vandalizing the Chinese quarters and intimidating the Chinese to prevent them from competing with white workers (Morton, 1974). There is evidence to indicate that during the period of agitation leading to the 1887 riot the mayor of Vancouver and some aldermen were at least sympathetic to the cause of keeping the Chinese out of the city (Roy, 1976, Morton, 1974). Many of the anti-Chinese rallies were held in the city hall with the permission of the council. The riot was serious enough that it prompted provincial Attorney-General Davie to introduce legislation appointing special constables in Vancouver and to suspend the judicial powers of the mayor, magistrates, and justices of the peace (Roy, 1976). Despite the passing of a special bill to preserve peace in Vancouver and the formation of a commission of inquiry later, only three people were charged with participating in the attack on the Chinese (Roy, 1976). Ironically, the bill was aimed not so much at protecting the Chinese as at salvaging the image of British Columbia; protecting the Chinese was, as Roy (1976: 58–9) put it, 'an incidental consequence'.

The public sentiment against the Chinese was again displayed in September, 1907. A parade organized by the Asiatic Exclusion League in Vancouver quickly turned into a riot (Morton, 1974). Among the slogans displayed on banners were these: 'A white Canada and no cheap Asiatic labor'; 'We have fought for the empire and are ready to fight again'; and 'White Canada—patronize your own race and Canada' (Morton, 1974: 203). As before, the crowd was against the alleged influx of Chinese and Japanese and their potential threat to job competition. In the minds of the rioters there was little doubt that patriotism meant defending a white Canada. The riot caused so much damage in Chinatown and the Japanese quarter that the federal government eventually had to strike a royal commission to investigate the losses sustained by the victims. Mackenzie King, the commissioner, finally recommended $26,990 in compensation payments for the losses of the Chinese (Royal Commission, 1907). There appears to have been little remorse after the riot, and anti-Chinese feelings remained strong. At a meeting of the Asiatic Exclusion League one participant, the Reverend Dr. Fraser, said, 'The action of the rioters has done more to impress upon the citizens of Canada the necessity of doing something than all the words spoken at the City Hall' (cited in Morton, 1974: 209).

Despite the small number of Chinese children in Canada, hostilities extended to the school system. Although there were only sixteen Chinese students attending the public schools in Victoria in 1901, the public sentiment was strong to segregate them from white students (Ashworth, 1979: 55). In 1902 the author of an article in the *Victoria Colonist* wrote:

The intermingling of Chinese children with children of Occidental parentage in the classrooms and playgrounds of the public schools is being called into question. . . . It is regrettable indeed that it should be found necessary to separate at the public schools the children of one portion of the inhabitants from the other for the preservation of the Anglo-Saxon standard of moral and ethical culture. But it is only carrying into the schools what already exists in every other institution of society—the branding of Chinese as Ishmaelites. (*Victoria Colonist*, Jan. 26, 1902, quoted in Ashworth, 1979: 58)

In 1908 the Victoria School Board accepted a recommendation to have separate classes for Chinese children (Ashworth, 1979: 73; Lee, 1967: 357), and in 1922 it decided to put all the Chinese students in one separate school. By that time there were 216 Chinese students in four city schools (Ashworth, 1979: 74). When the principals of these schools called out the Chinese students and marched them to King's Road School, the Chinese students and their parents started a boycott (Ashworth, 1979; Lee, 1967) that lasted a year, until the board permitted the Chinese students to return to the schools (Ashworth, 1979: 80).

The meaning of institutional racism

The discrimination against Chinese in virtually every sector of society cannot be easily dismissed as an historical accident, based purely on white Canadians' fear of a non-white minority. The removal of citizenship rights, the exclusion from immigration, and the restrictions on occupational competition were legally sanctioned by the state and thus formally institutionalized. The resulting discrimination was systematic and legal, and its practice was rationalized by an ideology stressing the superiority of white over non-white. It is on this basis that the term 'institutional racism' is appropriate, as distinct from individual racism, which may be manifested in various forms of prejudicial dispositions (see, for example, Hughes and Kallen, 1974: 105–8; Wellman, 1977: 39–44). According to Bolaria and Li (1985: 21), institutional racism involves both a racist theory and a social practice that are entrenched in institutions, and by which subordinate members are barred from equal participation.

From the point of view of employers and industrialists, institutional racism facilitates the exploitation of labour, especially during periods when the labour supply is erratic. One of the essential features of capitalist production is the ability of employers to divert the overhead cost of labour reproduction to the market, particularly during recessions (Pentland, 1959). This is accomplished by creating a versatile pool of reserve labour, which can furnish additional labour supply during industrial booms and absorb surplus labour during economic stagnations. The basic dilemma, then, is how to maintain the marginal status of a class of labour so that it can be used as a labour reserve capable of responding to uneven capitalist development. Institutional racism provides part of the answer. By removing the political and civil rights of a racial group, racist policies in essence restrict the bargaining power of the group vis-à-vis employers and other workers and thereby reduce the market value and social standing of the group being discriminated against. This in turn makes it possible to justify a split labour market (Bonacich, 1972, 1975), in which the price of labour is not the same for two racial groups performing the same tasks. It is an effective mechanism to ensure that menial tasks of industrial production are performed by a racial group at a relatively lower cost, even when white workers succeed in demanding higher wages. Over time, the low economic status of the racial group performing menial tasks further reinforces the social marginality of that group. It can easily be seen that an ideology defining a racial group as non-assimilable and inferior becomes useful, and indeed necessary, to rationalize racial exploitation. This explanation suggests that institutional racism against the Chinese was a structural imperative, given the dependence of many pioneer industries on cheap casual labour. It also suggests why superfical physical features, such as skin colour, can provide a convenient excuse for segregation and discrimination. When this happens, race ceases to be merely a primordial feature of people and takes on an objective reality that is at least in part defined by institutional inequality (Bolaria and Li, 1985).

There are strong legal grounds to indicate that discrimination against the Chinese was based on race and its stereotypical connotations. The laws to curtail their civil and political rights were aimed at the Chinese as a racial group. Since little consideration was given to those Chinese who were naturalized Canadians, the latter were subjected to the same anti-Chinese legislative bills as alien Chinese and were equally deprived of the basic rights of a Canadian. For example, the Chinese Immigration Act of 1923 clearly stipulated that the classification of persons of Chinese origin or descent was 'irrespective of allegiance or citizenship' (Statutes of Canada 1923, c. 38, s. 5). The Statutes of British Columbia were much more explicit in defining a 'Chinaman' according to race:

> Chinaman means any native of the Chinese Republic or its dependencies not born of British parents, and shall include any person of the Chinese race, naturalized or not. (Statutes of B. C. 1920, c. 27, s. 2.1)

Discrimination against naturalized Chinese-Canadians was in direct conflict with the Dominion Naturalization Act of 1914 with regard to the rights of naturalized subjects. Section 3 of the act stated:

> A person to whom a certificate of naturalization is granted by the Secretary of State of Canada . . . shall be entitled to all political and other rights, powers and privileges, and be subject to all obligations, duties and liabilities, to which a natural-born British subject is entitled or subject, and as from the date of his naturalization have to all intents and purposes the status of a natural-born British subject. (Statutes of Canada 1914, c. 44, s. 3)

Despite this conflict, the majority of the anti-Chinese bills were not legally challenged. Some were declared unconstitutional,[4] but only on the grounds that the Dominion, and not the provincial government, had the exclusive right to pass legislation pertaining to aliens and immigration. In the few cases where the Chinese tried to fight the discriminatory acts in court, their efforts met with little success. For example, in 1914 a Chinese restaurant owner in Moose Jaw, Saskatchewan, appealed to the Supreme Court of Canada claiming that his rights as a British subject were violated by the Saskatchewan act of 1912, which prohibited the hiring of white females by Chinese employers (*Quong-Wing v. The King*, Reports of the Supreme Court of Canada, 1914). The Supreme Court dismissed the appeal. Judge Davies explained his ruling as follows:

> There is no doubt in my mind that the prohibition is a racial one. . . . It extends and was intended to extend to all Chinamen as such, naturalized or aliens. . . . The Chinaman prosecuted in this case was found to have been born in China and of Chinese parents and, although, at the date of the offense charged, he had become a naturalized British subject, and had changed his political alle-

giance, he had not ceased to be a Chinaman within the meaning
of that word as used in the statute. . . . The prohibition against
the employment of white women was not aimed at alien Chinamen simply or at Chinamen having any political affiliations . . .
but at Chinamen as men of a particular race or blood, and whether
aliens or naturalized. (Supreme Court of Canada, 1914 [*Quong-
Wing v. The King*]: vol. 49, 449–50)

Through a series of legislative controls the Chinese in Canada,
and particularly in British Columbia, were reduced to second-
class citizens. In handing down the judgement in a case regarding the legal rights of orientals, the Supreme Court of Canada
was of the opinion that the provincial legislative acts in question

were in truth devised to deprive the Chinese, naturalized or not,
of the ordinary rights of the inhabitants of British Columbia and,
in effect, to prohibit their continued residence in that province,
since it prohibited their earning their living in that province.
(Canadian Reports, Appeal Cases, 1903 [*Cunningham v. Tomey
Homma*]: vol. 13, 151)

The same court, however, maintained that it was within the
power of the province to pass such acts.

Aside from the obvious economic interests of many industries
in maintaining a racialized labour force, there is evidence to suggest that some of the racial antagonism was aimed at eliminating
the competition for white workers from the Chinese. The
Chinese were tolerated as cheap labourers in menial jobs that
were not sought by white workers, but as soon as they ventured
into more desirable and higher-paying jobs they quickly became
the target of racial exclusion. It was in reaction to the tense competition between Chinese and white workers that the Royal Commission of 1902 concluded as follows:

Immigrants who come to other parts of Canada come to make it
their home and meet on an equal footing. In British Columbia this
normal condition of equal opportunity is disturbed by an immigration so different in kind, in civilization, in manner and cost of
living, that it puts the unskilled working man at a disadvantage
in every vocation in life where he meets this class of labour, and
he meets it everywhere. (Royal Commission, 1902: 276)

The concern over Chinese competition was also expressed by
many merchants' associations in British Columbia when they
learned that the proposed Chinese Immigration Act of 1923

included Chinese merchants under an admissible category of entry into Canada.[5] Prior to the second reading of the bill, the Retail Merchants' associations of Canada, Victoria, New Westminster, and Vernon sent telegrams to members of Parliament urging them to prevent Chinese merchants from entering Canada. A member of Parliament from Vernon named MacKelvie was forthright in telling the House that many people in his area were upset by the success of oriental vegetable-growers in the Okanagan Valley (Canada House of Commons Debates, 1923: 2322). Earlier, when Chinese miners began to compete with white miners for skilled jobs, the government of British Columbia responded to the demands of white miners by passing the Coal Mines Regulation Act of 1903, forbidding Chinese both to work underground and to occupy various skilled jobs in mines (Statutes of B. C. 1903, c. 17). But Chinese could continue to work as unskilled labourers above ground. Ironically, despite frequent complaints from white workers over the undesirability of Chinese labour, white workers were more than willing to hire Chinese when the former became small contractors (Royal Commission, 1885: xxx).

This apparently contradictory approach to Chinese labour is illustrated by the findings of the Royal Commissions of 1885 and 1902, in which the Chinese were regarded as racially undesirable but useful to the economy. Since there was an abundant supply of both white and Chinese labour, there was no need to maintain a large flow of Chinese into the country. Both commissions therefore recommended a head tax as a means of controlling future Chinese immigration to Canada. The tax resolved a basic dilemma: on the one hand, the desire to maintain the convenience of Chinese labour; on the other, an unwillingness to recognize the rights of Chinese as Canadians. It was a means of ensuring that the supply of Chinese labour would not be completely severed, while at the same time officially endorsing the second-class entrance status of the Chinese. This endorsement helped to sustain the marginal participation of the Chinese in the Canadian economy.

In addition to restricting immigration and thereby pacifying some of the anti-Chinese sentiment in British Columbia, the tax brought substantial financial gains for the government. Table 2.1 shows that between 1886 and 1943 the total revenue collected from the Chinese through head taxes and registrations to leave amounted to $23 million. Although the number of Chinese paying the head tax between 1905 and 1914 declined to 27,578 from 32,457 over the previous decade (1895–1904), the revenue increased six times, from $2.4 million to $13.8 million; this increase was due to a higher head tax of $500 as a result of the 1903 legislation. Between 1905 and 1914 alone the government collected $13.8 million from the Chinese.[6] This figure is equivalent to about 8 per cent of all excise duties collected in Canada, and about 14 per cent of the national defense budget, for this period.[7] But the number of Chinese in Canada accounted only for 0.39 per cent of the Canadian population in 1911, and 0.45 per cent in 1921 (Li, 1980: 64). The provincial government of British Columbia also benefited from the head tax, as one-quarter of it went to the province that collected it (Statutes of Canada, 1885, c. 71, s. 20; 1900, c. 32, s. 24). The 1903 Act increased the provincial share of the tax to one-half (Statutes of Canada, 1903, c. 8, sec. 24). It is also clear from Table 2.1 that the $500 head tax after 1903 only slowed down the inflow of Chinese immigrants. It was not until after the Chinese Immigration Act of 1924 that Chinese immigration to Canada was virtually halted.

TABLE 2.1

TOTAL REVENUE FROM HEAD TAX AND REGISTRATIONS FOR LEAVE OF CHINESE IMMIGRANTS, 1886–1943

Period	Number of Chinese paying head tax	Number of Chinese exempted from head tax	Number of Chinese registered for leave	Total revenue ($)
1886–1894	12,197	264	11,152	624,679
1895–1904	32,457	430	11,791	2,374,400
1905–1914[a]	27,578	4,458	33,833	13,845,977
1915–1924	10,147	2,807	50,111	5,678,865
1925–1934	2	5	48,127	473,564
1935–1943	0	1	9,938	52,061
Total	82,381	7,965	164,952	23,069,546

SOURCES: Compiled from *Canada Year Book*, 1931: 185 and 1941: 123; *Annual Report*, Canada Dept. of Mines and Resources, 1939–44.
[a]Figures for 1907 based on nine months.

Aside from the economic benefits that Chinese labour brought for the Canadian government and employers, anti-orientalism also served the interests of many groups. For example, union organizers and politicans used the issue of Chinese exclusion as a means of consolidating union organization as well as of winning political support. The organized-labour movement in Canada did not reach a national scale until the 1880s. Even then the trade-union movement in British Columbia had only limited support; except for 1918 and 1919 it enrolled only about 10 per cent of the non-agricultural labour force between 1911 and 1939 (Ward, 1980). In their desperation to enroll more workers, union organizers often used the Chinese question to recruit popular support. As Saywell (1951: 133) puts it: 'The Orientals became the scapegoat . . . and the blame for every malady was at one time or another placed upon them.' Much of the success of the Trades and Labour Congress of Canada in promoting a national union between 1880 and 1900 can be attributed to its anti-oriental policy, which tended to unify otherwise dissenting groups (Saywell, 1951). One author suggests that the Trades and Labour Congress originally incorporated a policy to exclude Chinese in its Platform of Principles in order to secure support from British Columbia representatives (Ireland, 1960). From 1899 onwards the congress reiterated an exclusion policy towards all Chinese in its annual conventions (Ireland, 1960).

Many politicians, too, were using the Chinese issue to advance their political careers. In 1879 Noah Shakespeare, a member of the Victoria City Council, formed the Anti-Chinese Association, and his platform to exclude the Chinese won him political success, first as mayor of Victoria, then as a member of Parliament (Woodsworth, 1941; Munro, 1971). Other politicians, like John Robson and Arthur Bunster, were actively using anti-Chinese issues to further their political stature in the provincial and federal legislatures (Morton, 1974, 43–5). By 1880 all political parties found it necessary to adopt an anti-Chinese stand in order to maintain popular support (Woodsworth, 1941).

From the treatment accorded the Chinese it is obvious that the anti-Chinese movement was propelled by many structural forces that were related to the economic and political development of western Canada. The antagonism towards the Chinese had little to do with alleged cultural differences of white Canadians and orientals, although the cultural argument was used time and again to justify the unequal treatment. In the following chapters we shall examine the effects of institutional racism on the Chinese community in Canada.

II

THE CHINESE COMMUNITY IN
THE EXCLUSION ERA

3

Occupations and Ethnic Business

By the time the Chinese Immigration Act of 1923 was passed, racism and discrimination against the Chinese were well entrenched in Canada's social structure. Between 1923 and 1947, Chinese were excluded by law from entering the country; during the same period the Chinese already in Canada were denied many citizenship rights. It is therefore appropriate to refer to those twenty-four years as the period of exclusion for the Chinese.

Institutional racism produced many disruptive effects on the life of the Chinese in Canada. Perhaps the most serious impact was on their economic life. The restriction on citizenship rights, together with the antagonism of white workers, placed the Chinese at a disadvantage in the labour market and jeopardized their ability to earn a living. Since the Chinese were singled out by law for unequal treatment, they carried a social stigma that labelled them as inferior. In this way the Chinese race in itself became convenient grounds for discrimination.

There were many ways in which the Chinese were discriminated against in the labour market. In those sectors where Chinese were hired along with white workers, they had to settle for lower wages. Indeed, lower wages became the incentive for white employers to hire Chinese, despite periodic protests from white workers. But as anti-orientalism intensified, the Chinese found themselves excluded by law from many industries that their cheap labour had previously helped to build. Racial hostility and legal barriers made it increasingly difficult for the Chinese to compete with white workers in the core labour market. Eventually, many Chinese retreated into the ethnic business sector, largely the service industry, where they found refuge by avoiding competition with white employers and workers.

Chinese labourers in a split labour market

There is evidence to suggest that the labour market in British

Columbia, at least up to 1900, was split by race in such a way that Chinese workers received, in many instances, about half the wage of white workers.[1] In some industries, such as coal mining and railroad maintenance, the only jobs the Chinese were allowed to perform were those that required lower skills and carried lower pay. In other industries, such as line-assembly manufacturing, Chinese and white workers performed the same jobs but received unequal pay.

Table 3.1 provides some evidence of the differential wage scales applied to Chinese and white workers around 1900. Although these are gross estimates, the figures show a consistent pattern of lower prices for Chinese than for white labour.[2] While white agricultural labourers earned $30 to $40 a month, Chinese farm labourers made about $20 to $25; Chinese cigar makers received 50 cents to $1.00 for making 100 cigars, as compared with $1.10 to $1.90 for white workers. The wages of Chinese coal miners, lumber and cannery workers, bootmakers, and sewing-machine operators were about half those of white labour, or less.

The differential wage system for Chinese and white workers

TABLE 3.1

WAGES OF CHINESE AND WHITE LABOUR BY SELECTED
OCCUPATIONS IN BRITISH COLUMBIA, CANADA,
AROUND 1900

Selected Occupation	Wage period	Wage of Chinese labour ($)	Wage of white labour ($)
Agricultural labourers	month	20–25	30–40
Bootmakers	day	1–1.35	2–3
Brickmakers	day	1.60	2–2.50
Cannery workers	month	40–50	80.91
Cigar makers	(per 100)	0.50–1	1.10–1.90
Coal miners	day	1.25	3–4
Lumber workers	day	1.25	2.25–3.75
Placer miners	day	2–2.25	3–3.50
Railway section men	day	1	1.25–1.50
Sewing-machine operators	month	10–25	40
Shingle workers	day	1.67	2.58

SOURCES: Figures based on testimony and evidence provided by employers in various industries (Royal Commission, 1902: 44–197).

appears to have been maintained as late as the 1930s. For example, in 1934 the Board of Industrial Relations in British Columbia devised a minimum-wage system for the province's saw-mill industry, which set the general wage at 35 cents an hour. But the system also allowed for up to 25 per cent of the total number of plant employees to be paid 25 cents an hour, and in practice oriental labourers were assigned to this lower-wage group. Government officials argued that even though it was lower than for others, the wage of 25 cents was in most cases a considerable increase for oriental workers. (Woodsworth, 1941: 142).

The testimonies of employers before the Royal Commission of 1902 indicate that the system of unequal wages benefited white workers: cheaper wages for Chinese workers meant a lower cost of production for employers in Canada and a better position for competition with producers in the United States. Without cheap Chinese labour, employers would have to either raise the price of their commodity or cut profits; the first solution was constrained by market competition, while the latter was not usually accepted by employers. As the manager of the Wellington Colliery Company explained to the Commission:

> If Chinese and Japs were not available we would have to get more for our coal or have to stop mining. The margin is close. . . . The Chinese are absolutely necessary for present work. The cost of production would be greater without the Chinese, but falling off in production here would not affect the price in San Francisco. It would compel us to reduce the white man's wage. (Royal Commission, 1902: 79)

From the point of view of employers, therefore, it was precisely because the Chinese were paid less that white workers were paid more. In this way both the profit margin of production and the higher wages of white workers were maintained by the cheap labour cost of the Chinese. Institutional racism and legislative controls provided justifications for the system of wage inequality.

Despite frequent allegations by white workers, there is little evidence that Chinese labour was competing directly with white labour prior to the 1880s. On the contrary, the employment of Chinese as unskilled labourers probably made it easier for white workers to take higher-status jobs in the skilled-labour sector. In the coal mines, for example, Chinese were frequently hired not as miners but as helpers to white miners (Royal Commission, 1902: 71–90). Likewise, in placer mining the Chinese took up only gold fields that had been abandoned by white miners (Royal Commission, 1902: 90–3).[3]

By the time the CPR was completed, employers and contractors had begun to use Chinese labourers as scabs to break strikes. Although many of the complaints against the Chinese by union workers were gross exaggerations,[4] in many instances the management profited from using Chinese as strike-breakers; Robert Dunsmuir, owner of a number of mines at Wellington, introduced several hundred Chinese workers to his mines as a means of settling the strikes in 1883 (Con, et al., 1982: 50). In 1903 the Western Federation of Miners suffered a heavy setback in its attempts to mobilize a series of strikes in British Columbia because the management imported oriental strike-breakers to the Nanaimo mines (Saywell, 1951). These measures on the part of employers, together with growing unemployment among Chinese after 1884, provoked further white working-class resentment towards the Chinese. The Knights of Labour formed in Victoria in 1884, were active in promoting anti-Chinese legislation (Morton, 1974: 111), and white miners in Nanaimo, Wellington, and Comox collected 1,421 petitions in 1891, and 2,700 petitions in 1892, to protest against hiring Chinese in coal mines (Woodsworth, 1941: 41). By the turn of the century many unions were barring Chinese from membership and demanding their total exclusion from the country (Saywell, 1951; Ireland, 1960).

Occupational patterns under exclusion

Historically, the split labour market was a structural arrangement in which white workers and employers accepted non-white workers (Bonacich, 1979). But as the lower wages of non-white workers began to displace the higher wages of white workers, the latter turned to racial exclusion as a means of monopolizing higher-paying jobs. Through job closure and job ghettoization, certain racial groups were restricted to only marginal participation in the economy. Under these conditions the working class is typically fractionalized by racial divisions (Miles, 1982) and class solidarity is confounded with racial antagonism. Indeed, as Ward (1980) points out, the major cleavages in British Columbia between 1870 and 1939 were based on race, not class.

The historical evidence indicates that as anti-orientalism among the white working class intensified, politicians were compelled to pass measures restricting the employment of Chinese and employers were forced to heed the demands of the populace. Eventually the Chinese lost their right to work in many fields and were tolerated only in the limited number of jobs for which few white workers would compete. Table 3.2 shows the occupational patterns of the Chinese in 1885, 1901, 1921, and 1931.

TABLE 3.2

OCCUPATIONS OF CHINESE IN BRITISH COLUMBIA (1885), VICTORIA (1901), AND CANADA (1921, 1931)

Occupation	1885[a] %	1901[b] %	1921[c] %	1931[d] %
Professional occupations	0.5	—	0.4	0.3
Store owners and merchants	1.3	9.2	4.6	3.6
Restaurant-keepers[e]	0.1	9.3	6.2	8.9
Laundry owners and managers	—	—	9.6	2.2
Farmers and gardeners	1.3	6.5	3.2	4.2
Miners	15.8	—	0.4	1.0
Food canners	7.6	29.1	0.2	0.8
Lumbermen and sawmill workers	7.6	1.6	3.2	1.6
Railroad workers	31.3	—	0.8	0.3
Store employees	3.3	—	2.2	1.9
Servants, cooks, and waiters	3.0	17.4	23.3	26.2
Laundry workers	1.7	6.5	9.0	13.6
Farm labourers	17.4	—	6.5	7.5
Other labourers	3.3	26.7	24.4	21.4
Other occupations	5.9	2.8	6.0	6.5
Total	100.1	100.1	100.1	100.1
(Total number of Chinese in labour force)	(9,272)	(3,042)	(34,042)	(40,253)

[a]Compiled from occupations of Chinese in B.C. (Royal Commission, 1885, Appendix C, pp. 363–5).
[b]Compiled from occupations of Chinese in Victoria (Royal Commission, 1902, pp. 12, 22).
[c]Census of Canada, 1931, vol. VII, table 69, pp. 988–97, including all gainfully employed Chinese in Canada, 10 years of age and over.
[d]Census of Canada, 1931, vol. VII, table 49, pp. 430–43, including all gainfully employed Chinese in Canada, 10 years of age and over.
[e]The figure for 1921 includes hotel and restaurant keepers.

The figures for 1885[5] indicate that they were concentrated in a number of labour-intensive industries—31 per cent in railroad work and almost 16 per cent in mining—while a large proportion were in farming (17.4 per cent) and other unskilled jobs (3.3 per cent). Taken together, these few job categories constituted about 70 per cent of the Chinese labour force in 1885.

The completion of the CPR meant that many Chinese were laid off, and a large number of them moved to the urban areas of British Columbia where they formed an unemployed labour pool (Morton, 1974: 136–137; Roy, 1976: 46). Much of this idle labour was probably taken up by the expanding manufacturing and canning industries in British Columbia. The prosperity of the salmon-canning industry, beginning around 1880, depended heavily on Chinese labour (Campbell, 1969: 37, 55). Table 3.2 shows that 7.6 per cent of the Chinese in the labour force, or 700 workers, were employed in food canning in Victoria in 1885.[6] By 1901 the number of Chinese engaged in the canning industry was estimated at around 6,000 (Royal Commission, 1902: 135).

Between 1885 and 1931 some major shifts took place in the occupational patterns of the Chinese. Whereas in 1885 farm and other labourers together constituted about 21 per cent of the Chinese labour force, by 1921 that percentage had increased to about 30 per cent (farm labourers 6.5 per cent; other labourers 24.4 per cent). This pattern persisted in 1931, with farm labourers making up 7.5 per cent, and other labourers another 21.4 per cent. In contrast, food canners decreased from 7.6 per cent in 1885 to 3.2 per cent in 1921 and 1.6 per cent in 1931. The number of miners among the Chinese dropped from 15.8 per cent in 1885 to 0.4 per cent in 1921 and 1.0 per cent in 1931. These changes indicate both the persistence of the Chinese in the unskilled labour sector and their gradual exclusion from the manufacturing occupations in which they had previously gained a foothold. These figures are also consistent with the argument that institutional racism limited the bargaining power of the Chinese and confined them to marginal participation in the labour market.

Another consequence of institutional exclusion was that it gave impetus to the development of ethnic businesses among the Chinese. The emergence of small businesses such as Chinese laundries and restaurants may be viewed as a survival adaptation, a way of developing alternative economic opportunities within a hostile labour market. Table 3.2 shows that in 1885 the number of Chinese engaged in laundry and restaurant work was less than 5 per cent (servants, cooks and waiters, 3 per cent; laundry workers, 1.7 per cent). By 1921, servants, cooks, waiters, and laundry workers made up 32 per cent, and by 1931, 40 per cent. The corresponding figures for laundry and restaurant owners were 0.1 per cent for 1885; 9.3 per cent for 1901; 15.8 per cent for 1921; and 11.1 per cent for 1931. These figures indicate the rising importance of ethnic businesses among Chinese as racial animosity compelled them to retreat into the ethnic enclave. Undoubtedly the ethnic businesses provided some Chinese with an opportunity for upward mobility that was not available in the non-ethnic sector.

The evidence of the United States indicates a similar pattern of development among the Chinese. As racial hostility forced them to leave the skilled occupations, they too entered the laundry and restaurant businesses (Li, 1976). The reason the laundry business flourished among the Chinese was that it was one of the few occupations that was noncompetitive with white labour and, at the same time, accepted by the dominant society (Li, 1978). Siu (1953: 23–5) suggests that as laundrymen the Chinese occupied a low economic status that was consistent with the image of an inferior race and hence accepted by white customers.

The Canadian evidence also suggests that the Chinese were tolerated as long as they were confined to subservient labour and the ethnic sector. Once they began to venture into the non-ethnic sector, and thereby compete with white workers and employers, anti-Chinese sentiment emerged. At the hearings of the Royal Commission of 1902 the Chinese were spoken of highly as domestic servants, while their presence in other industries was vehemently opposed (Royal Commission, 1902: 167–72). Similarly in Vancouver, in 1928, as the number of Chinese retail business began to increase outside Chinatown, the Retail Merchants and the Canadian Manufacturers' Association initiated a campaign to curb the spread of Chinese into the city's business community (Morton, 1974: 244). The same pattern was repeated in 1936 when some Chinese moved into wholesale market-gardening in Vancouver (Morton, 1974: 245–8).

The hostile job market for the Chinese was well summarized by the Reverend Osterhout of the United Church, Superintendent of the Oriental Missions West of the Great Lakes:

> The chief difficulties arise as the [Chinese] graduates from high school and universities emerge into commercial life. Here discrimination is marked. . . . There are few industries which are open to them except those carried on among themselves, such as the green grocer stores, Oriental shops, laundries and cafes. (Cited in Chow, 1976: 122)

Even the few Chinese-Canadians with higher education were not immune from market discrimination. As one Chinese described the experience before the war:

> Among the Canadian-born Chinese, there were a few of us who went to university. Some of them, like my two brothers, got their degrees at University of British Columbia. But none of them was able to find work. One of my brothers was a civil engineer, who graduated in 1933. He wasn't able to get anything, so he had to go to Quebec. . . . My other brother got a degree in dairying. He wasn't able to find anything, so he went back to China around 1935. (Interview transcripts, quoted in Li, 1982: 532)

Economic opportunities were so limited that there was a sense of hopelessness even for the better-educated Chinese. Woodsworth quoted a Chinese university graduate:

> There is no choice for the young people here as to what they will do, it's just a matter of taking whatever turns up or remaining idle. . . . After many repeated setbacks they feel disgusted and give up hope. The situation as it stands, where young people live in a state of shattered hopes and ambitions, is deplorable because instead of an aggressive, quick-thinking bunch of Chinese-Canadian youths, one finds a submissive, fatalistic group of young people. . . . The opportunity for university students is no greater. . . . If they remain too long after graduation in this country, they also begin to resign themselves to their fate and lose their ambition. (Quoted in Woodsworth, 1941: 150)

The economic exclusion of the Chinese persisted at least until after the Second World War. The growth of ethnic business among the Chinese in Canada in the 1920s and 1930s reflected their successful attempt to establish an economic niche by avoiding competition with white workers and business people.

As the Chinese retreated from many industries and entered the ethnic business sector there was a corresponding change in the concentration of the Chinese population. Up until 1891 nearly all the Chinese in Canada were concentrated in British Columbia (Table 3.3). The intensification of racial hostility and economic exclusion in the province probably had the effect of dispersing some Chinese to other provinces. As Table 3.3 indicates, the percentage distribution of Chinese in British Columbia declined after 1901, and by 1931 only 58 per cent of the Chinese in Canada resided there. There is little indication that the job opportunities for Chinese were better in other provinces; available data suggest that the hostility elsewhere (see Palmer, 1970; Hoe, 1976) was similar to that experienced by Chinese in British Columbia. As the Chinese population in other parts of Canada rose, however, the number of Chinese businesses also increased. In Calgary, for example, there were five Chinese laundries in 1901, and by 1922 there were forty-eight laundries, seven cafés, and fifteen Chinese groceries (Hoe, 1976: 74).

TABLE 3.3

DISTRIBUTION OF CHINESE POPULATION IN CANADA, 1881–1941

Province	1881 %	1891 %	1901 %	1911 %	1921 %	1931 %	1941 %
British Columbia	99	98	86	70	59	58	54
Ontario	1	1	4	10	14	15	18
Quebec	—	—	6	6	6	6	7
Alberta	—	—	1	6	9	8	9
Saskatchewan	—	—	—	4	7	8	7
Manitoba	—	—	1	3	3	4	4
Maritimes and Territories[a]	—	1	1	1	1	1	2
Total	100	100	99	100	99	100	101
(Number of Chinese)	(4,383)	(9,129)	(17,314)	(27,831)	(39,587)	(46,519)	(34,627)

SOURCES: Figures for 1881 and 1891 compiled from Dept. of Agriculture, 1893: 133–4. Figures for 1901–41 compiled from Census of Canada, 1941, vol. 1, *General Review and Summary Tables*, tables 32–3, pp. 684–92.
[a]Nova Scotia, New Brunswick, Prince Edward Island, Yukon, and Northwest Territories.

The social organization of Chinese businesses

Sociologists use the term 'ethnic business' to refer to the type of business organizations associated with an ethnic community, as characterized by small firms, owned and operated by minority members, that are located in a limited number of specialized markets, such as retailing and food services (Bonacich and Modell, 1980; Auster and Aldrich, 1984; Ward and Jenkins, 1984). The operations of ethnic businesses are usually small and labour-intensive. Although competition is not likely to come from non-ethnic entrepreneurs, intra-ethnic competition within the community can be severe. Often ethnic entrepreneurs rely on family members and kin for a continuous supply of unpaid or underpaid labour. The low cost of labour reduces operating expenses and enables ethnic businesses to survive through periods of recession.

Many of the above characteristics can be seen in the business operations of the Chinese in the 1930s. At first many entered the laundry business. But as the market for hand laundry declined they moved into the restaurant business and other retail operations in urban centres. Aside from limited census data, it is difficult to estimate the extent of Chinese business before the war. According to one source, by 1924 there were 14,000 Chinese in the laundry business and 9,000 in the restaurant business (Cheng, 1931: 196). The total number of Chinese in the Canadian labour force was 34,042 in 1921 and 40,253 in 1931 (Table 3.2).

There is little doubt that discrimination and exclusion provided the structural conditions for the emergence of ethnic business among the Chinese (Li, 1976, 1979a). But their success in small businesses also reflects their ability to overcome resource limitations and market barriers by developing those cultural elements that could assist them in their entrepreneurial ventures.

In a study of ethnic business among the Chinese in Canada between 1910 and 1947, Li (1982) conducted extensive interviews with elderly Chinese to find out what the Chinese restaurants were like at that time and what the social background of the operators was. Unlike the Chinese restaurants that burgeoned after the war in the urban centres, these early Chinese restaurants were small in scale, poorly decorated, and labour-intensive. The operators were largely working-class people with a history of

transient employment in various marginal jobs, as the following
case history illustrates:

> I came to Moose Jaw in 1913. . . . First I washed dishes, making
> $35 a month. I worked for fourteen to sixteen hours a day. I knelt
> down on the floor and washed the floor and washed the dining
> room every morning. I had a potato bag to make it easier for my
> knees. Then after that, I went to Simpson, at harvest time, up
> north, it was the CPR line. I worked on a farm. I got up at six
> o'clock in the morning, milked the cow, and came back to the
> house to cook breakfast for my boss. . . . He was not a very
> friendly person. . . . It was no good, so I quit. I came back to
> Moose Jaw to work for my brother for $50 a month for twelve
> hours a day. At night I scrubbed the floor and waited on tables.
> Then in 1918 I went back to China to get married. (Interview
> transcripts , cited in Li, 1982: 533)

These Chinese entered the restaurant business basically as a
means of creating self-employment, especially when it was difficult for them to find any other jobs. In many cases they were
doing the same kinds of work in their own restaurants as they
did when working for somebody else. The operators had to put
in long hours in order to maintain a low profit margin. The harsh
life was described by one Chinese:

> As long as you had a place to sleep and some work, then it didn't
> matter. In the winter time it was cold and there were no people
> there. Some days we had only a few people, just sold a few loaves
> of bread and a few cups of coffee, that's all. No, it didn't matter
> as long as you had a place to stay. (Ibid.: 535)

As well as requiring only a small capital investment, the restaurant business had low risks and provided a means of survival in
hard economic times. During the Depression the restaurants provided a refuge for many Chinese. As one described the situation
during the early thirties:

> There were four partners and ten others who just stayed there.
> . . . There was no work to do elsewhere, and they looked after
> the restaurant. (Ibid.)

Although the initial investment to start a restaurant could be as
low as a few hundred dollars, given the kinds of jobs most
Chinese had, their capacity to save that much money was limited.

Many resorted to partnerships, pooling their limited resources to finance the operation. The business partners would then work as a team in running the restaurant to reduce the cost of hiring other workers. The following excerpts suggest how a partnership business was formed and conducted:

> The partners get a few relatives together and just chip in some money, that's all. . . . Every day . . . fixed meals, cooked the meat, made a few pies, and made some soup. Whatever we needed we made it. . . . There was no boss. Everyone did it right. That was the way we did it. Just worked for ourselves. In the end, whoever had a share had a share of the profit . . . If you really don't like it and can't get along, then you can buy me out, or I can buy you out. (Ibid.)

Partnerships were usually made on an informal basis, without legal arrangements. This system seems to have been widely accepted among the Chinese. As one explained:

> Get a few relatives together, and each just chip in together. You don't need a lawyer, and you don't have to sign, just take each other's word. . . . If he is a good man or if he is your cousin then you would be his partner. . . . In the old days . . . we all worked partnerships. (Ibid.: 536)

Leaving a partnership was as simple as forming one. Often the withdrawal was prompted more by personal than by business reasons. The following case is an example:

> I sold it [the partnership] and went to China. There were about seven or eight of us there. They were my cousins, and so I sold my part of my business to them. So then when I came back, the restaurant was busy, and they asked me to stay and work for them. I worked for three or four months, and they asked me to become a partner [again]. (Ibid.: 535)

A number of factors probably facilitated the formation of business partnerships among the Chinese immigrants. Since the Chinese emigrated largely from the same region, common lineage and clanship ties, in the absence of other resources, provided a pool of potential partners with whom business relationships could be formed. Indeed, partnerships were frequently formed between fathers and sons, uncles and nephews, and brothers. In some cases the partnership might be extended to more distant relatives and friends. In this way distant kinship ties that might otherwise have been ignored became instrumental in business ventures.

Business partners were not only co-investors, but also co-workers in the same café or restaurant; it was just as necessary for them to pool their labour as their capital. Since the meagre return from operating a restaurant required using unpaid labour to reduce the operating cost, most Chinese partners had to rely on each other, especially in the absence of their wives and children. Thus, ironically, the separation of the Chinese men from their families in China facilitated the formation of business partnerships. Such partnerships declined after the war, when the new immigration policy allowed more Chinese to bring their families to Canada. The family members provided additional labour to operate the restaurant, and many partnerships broke up as the demographic pattern of the Chinese community changed.

4

Marriage and the Family

Despite the popular belief that the traditional Chinese family was large and complex, there is no evidence to indicate that the Chinese-Canadian family resembles that image. In fact, traditional Chinese familism has had little to do with the development of the Chinese-Canadian family. Except in isolated cases, the Chinese-Canadian family did not emerge until after the Second World War. Most Chinese men in Canada before the war were denied a conjugal family life and were forced to live in a predominantly married-bachelor society. The patterns of broken families among Chinese males in Canada and the consequent disruption in social life can be attributed to the anti-Chinese policy and hostile social environment, which imposed various legal and social constraints on familial organization. The anti-oriental policy of the Canadian government over an extended period produced long-term effects on the Chinese community, the consequences of which were evident even long after the restrictive measures were removed. The post-war changes, notably the removal of legislative exclusion of Chinese immigrants to Canada, enabled the reunion of some Chinese family members. Subsequent amendments to the Immigration Act gradually allowed the immigration of Chinese families to Canada.

The traditional Chinese family: myth and reality

The effects of Confucianism on overseas Chinese families have often been overstated. Chan (1983: 103), for example, claims that historically Confucianism 'remained pure in theory and application' among the Chinese in Canada, and that its ideology exerted a strong influence, as shown in the patriarchal family. While there is little evidence to support this viewpoint, there are many grounds to believe that the most common image of the traditional Chinese family is false.

That image depicts the traditional family as a large patriarchal system characterized by a complex structure in which several generations live under the same roof. Such a structure is widely believed to have been popular and economically viable in mainland China at least until the nineteenth century and possibly until the early part of the twentieth. Kinship ties are seen as the fundamental relationships in Chinese society, and their importance was reinforced by the pseudo-religious precepts of Confucianism.

These misconceptions are largely due to confusion at various conceptual levels. First, there is a profound difference between the ideals of traditional familism, as incorporated in the ethical precepts of neo-Confucianism, and the form of the Chinese family as an empirical reality. The Confucian values of filial piety, domestic harmony, and ancestor worship represented a political view that facilitated the social control held by the state (Freedman, 1961–62). Proponents of Confucianism came from the aristocracy (Ho, 1965). Although over time its family-oriented values were disseminated among the Chinese masses, China has remained a land of small families since the collapse of the feudal system in the fourth century B.C. (Ho, 1965). Second, the Chinese family varied in form according to region and social origin. The vast territory of rural hinterlands meant that the majority of the population belonged to the peasantry, while the minority, the gentry, was based mainly in urban centres. The difference between the gentry family and the peasant family was one of both status and resources. Third, a distinction should be drawn between the natural family and the organized clan, the latter being at best marginal to the economic life of the Chinese since its emergence in the eleventh century (Ho, 1965).

Because supporting a large and complex family requires a certain level of material affluence, historically such a structure was possible only among the Chinese gentry (Fei, 1946). In terms of population, the gentry as a social class would exclude over 90 per cent of the country's people, the majority of whom belonged to the peasantry. The family unit at this level was numerically small and structurally simple (Freedman, 1961–62; Ho, 1965). Economic necessity compelled both the husband and the wife to participate actively and jointly in agricultural production. The ideology of patriarchy operated much more weakly at this level of familial organization than among high-status families.

That the traditional Chinese family was small in size is supported by substantial empirical evidence. Ho (1965), for example, reports the average size of the Chinese households as 5.96 in A.D. 755, 5.68 in 1393, 5.33 in 1812, and about 5 for the first half of the twentieth century. In other words, the size of the average Chinese household has been declining for the last 1,200 years, since long before the advent of modern industrialization. These statistics suggest that, contrary to what patriarchy and Confucianism would lead one to predict, the economic conditions of life in China limited the family to a size similar to that of the nuclear family in the twentieth-century industrialized nations. They further suggest that extended familism was at best an ideal of neo-Confucianism, which might have been realized only among a few of gentry origin.

Studies of Chinese communities in Southeast Asia indicate that whatever influence extended familism may have had in China, it was not transplanted overseas (Hoe, 1976: 265–6). The structure of the nuclear family was the rule, not an exception, among the Chinese in Singapore, North Borneo, Thailand, and other parts of Southeast Asia. Only in rare cases were joint families found among the wealthy (Hoe, 1976).

Historical patterns of the Chinese-Canadian family

Very few of the Chinese who came to Canada during the nineteenth century brought their families with them. With the exception of some merchants who could afford to do so, the immigrants were young adult males who came singly. Before the end of the Second World War conjugal family life among the Chinese-Canadians was rare, and the Chinese community consisted predominantly of married bachelors who sent remittances to support their families in China (Hoe, 1976).

With respect to the merchants, the historical statistics available indicate that they made up only a small fraction of the Chinese in Canada and that not all of them brought their wives. For example, of the Chinese entering Canada between 1885 and 1903 only 5 per cent were merchants, and less than 1 per cent were wives (see Table 1.1). In 1902 there were 92 wives among the 3,263 Chinese in Victoria, 61 of whom were married to merchants, and 28 to labourers (Royal Commission, 1902: 13). Among the 76 Chinese families in Victoria in 1902 the average

number of people in each was about 4.1.[1] This small family size
would rule out the likelihood of extended familism even among
the merchant class in Canada. In Vancouver, the same year, there
were 2,053 Chinese men and 27 Chinese women, of whom 16
were wives of merchants, 8 of labourers, 1 of a minister, and 2
of interpreters (Royal Commission, 1902: 13). The census figures
of later years also indicate that merchants and store-owners com-
prised a small proportion of the Chinese: in 1921 they accounted
for 4.6 per cent of the employed Chinese, and in 1931, 3.6 per
cent (Table 3.2). These statistics suggest that even the so-called
merchant families were rare at best, and that extended familism
could not have existed among them on a large scale, given the
small average family size.

It is sometimes argued that immigrants are unwilling to identify with the host society because of a sojourner orientation (see,
for example, Siu, 1953; Li, 1976), which would also, according
to the argument, explain their reluctance to immigrate with their
families. In the case of the Chinese in Canada there is little evidence to support this explanation. Economic hardship and social
hostility deterred many Chinese from bringing their wives and
children in the period prior to the Chinese Immigration Act of
1923, when it was still legally possible to sponsor them. The same
economic factors that compelled many to leave China in the first
place also prevented them from paying for the passage of family
members. The cost of bringing a family member increased substantially after 1885, when the $50 head tax was imposed on
practically every Chinese entering Canada. This tax was raised
to $100 in 1900, and $500 in 1903. Most Chinese probably had
difficulty raising the money for their own entry, let alone that for
family members.

Aside from the financial cost, there were social costs too that
tended to discourage the Chinese from bringing their families.
Hostilities and discrimination often led to abuses and attacks.
The Chinese quarters and enclaves were frequent targets of racial
harassment, as in the anti-oriental riots of 1887 and 1907 in Vancouver (Roy, 1976; Morton, 1974). The apprehension of the
Chinese was well summarized by a witness who testified before
the 1902 commission:

> A large proportion of them would bring their families here were
> it not for the unfriendly reception they got here during recent

years, which creates an unsettled feeling. (Royal Commission, 1902: 2326)

The Chinese Immigration Act of 1923 excluded all Chinese from immigrating. Until its repeal, in 1947, it was legally impossible for many wives in China to join their husbands in Canada. This legal barrier further reinforced the sex imbalance in the Chinese-Canadian community, which was the highest among ethnic groups in Canada (Li, 1980a). In 1911 the ratio of Chinese men to 100 Chinese women was 2,790 (see Table 4.2), while the corresponding sex ratio for all Canada was 113 men to 100 women (Li, 1980a: 65). In other words, the sex imbalance among the

TABLE 4.1

AGE AND SEX OF CHINESE IMMIGRANTS ADMITTED
ANNUALLY TO CANADA, 1907–24

	Adults		Children	Total	
Year	Male %	Female %	%	%	Number
1907	68.5	9.8	21.7	100.0	92
1908	91.2	2.1	6.7	100.0	1884
1909	89.8	1.9	8.3	100.0	1887
1910	86.5	2.7	10.8	100.0	2156
1911	92.1	1.5	6.5	100.1	5278
1912	92.5	1.3	6.3	100.1	6247
1913	94.4	1.1	4.4	99.9	7445
1914	94.9	1.6	3.5	100.0	5512
1915	91.2	3.2	5.6	100.0	1258
1916	47.7	20.5	31.8	100.0	88
1917	75.6	8.4	16.0	100.0	393
1918	90.4	3.4	6.2	100.0	769
1919	94.5	1.5	4.0	100.0	4333
1920	71.5	12.3	16.2	100.0	544
1921	82.2	5.5	12.3	100.0	2435
1922	64.4	6.5	29.0	99.9	1746
1923	32.6	8.3	59.1	100.0	711
1924	8.8	5.3	85.9	100.0	674

SOURCES: Compiled from annual reports of the Dept. of the Interior (1906–17) and Dept. of Immigration and Colonization (1918–24). Data based on those immigrants of Chinese nationality tabulated by fiscal year ending March 31. Figures for 1907 based on nine months.

Chinese was about 25 times the national figure. Although the census figures regarding the sex ratio before 1911 are not available, one would expect a similar imbalance in the preceding years, given the social hostility and federal legal controls in place since 1885. According to the immigration data on Chinese admitted between 1906 and 1924, the ratio was 3,578 men to 100 women (Li, 1980a: 62). Table 4.1 shows in greater detail the distribution of men, women, and children by year for the period 1907 to 1924. Except for 1916 and 1920, the number of Chinese women admitted each year was well below 10 per cent. Table 4.1 also shows

TABLE 4.2

SEX RATIO AND NATIVITY OF CHINESE IN CANADA, 1881-1981

Year	Total number of Chinese in Canada	Males per 100 females	Native-born %
1881	4,383	—	0
1891	9,129	—	0
1901	17,312	—	—
1911	27,831	2,790	3
1921	39,587	1,533	7
1931	46,519	1,241	12
1941	34,627	785	20
1951	32,528	374	31
1961	58,197	163	40
1971	118,815	112	38
1981	289,245	102	25

SOURCES: Compiled from Censuses of Canada: 1911, *Special Report on the Foreign-Born Population*, table 22, p. 50; 1911, vol. II, table XII, pp. 368–9; 1921, vol. I, *Population*, table 29, pp. 560–3; 1931, vol. XIII, *Racial Origins and Nativity of the Canadian People* (W. Burton Hurd), table 16, p. 768; 1931, vol. I, *Summary*, inserted table, between pp. 234–5; 1941, vol. I, *General Review and Summary Tables*, tables 35–6, pp. 694–7; 1951, vol. I, *Population, General Characteristics*, table 31, p. 31:1; 1951, vol. II, *Population*, table 37, p. 37:1; 1961, vol. I, part 2, series 1.2, bulletin 1.2–5, *Population, Ethnic Groups*, table 35, pp. 35:1–35:2; 1961, vol. II, part I, bulletin 7.1–6, *Origins of the Canadian Population*, table XVII, p. 6:38; 1971, vol. I, part 2, bulletin 1.3–2, *Population, Ethnic Groups*, table 3, pp. 3:1–3:2; 1971, *Public Use Sample Tape, Individual File*, special computation; 1981, vol. I, *Population, Ethnic Origin*, table 1, pp. 1:1–1:22; 1981, *A User's Guide to 1981 Census Data on Ethnic Origin* (Walton O. Boxhill), table 8, pp. 32–6.

that in the few years prior to 1923, when the Chinese Immigration Act was passed, there was an increase in the percentage of children admitted. This upsurge reflected the anticipation of the restrictive immigration act on the part of the Chinese and their efforts to bring in some of their children before the law came into effect.

Throughout the twenties and thirties Chinese males outnumbered females by 12 to 15 times. Table 4.2 shows that the sex ratio was 1,533 men to 100 women in 1921, and 1,241 to 100 in 1931. The corresponding sex ratio per 100 females for all of Canada during this period was 106 in 1921 and 107 in 1931 (Li, 1980a: 65). Despite a general decline in the unbalanced sex ratio among the Chinese over the census years, it remained relatively high: 785 in 1941 and 374 in 1951. In the post-war period the sex ratio steadily declined. But it was not until 1981 that it began to approach an equilibrium. For the period between 1921 and 1951 the improvement towards a more balanced sex ratio may have been due partly to a decline in the male population as many left Canada, and partly to a modest increase in Canadian-born Chinese. The more balanced sex ratio in 1951 (374 males to 100 females) reflected the change in the immigration law of 1947, which lifted the Chinese exclusion and thereby made it possible for some wives to join their husbands in Canada.

Married life in separation

During the period of legislative exclusion, 1923 to 1947, many married Chinese men in Canada had to live apart from their wives in China. Even before the 1923 act came into effect it was unusual among the Chinese to have a family in Canada. The testimonies of both Caucasian and Chinese witnesses appearing before the 1902 Royal Commission provide some insight into the family structure at that time. As one Caucasian witness testified:

> Very few of the Chinese have families here, only three or four of them have. I don't think they send very much to China; they save for a while and make a trip home and most of them come back.
> (Royal Commission, 1902: 77)

Married life was often just as transient as the marriage itself, which often took place during a hasty trip to China. After the marriage these men would return to Canada until they could afford another trip home (Hoe, 1976: 269–75). For many it meant a long period of separation from their families. Regular remittances were sent to China by these married bachelors to support their families. For those who were economically more successful there were occasional trips home for a year or, at most, two before returning to Canada, as the law prevented them from being away for more than two years without losing the right to return (Statutes of Canada 1923, c. 38, s. 24). For many, however, the dream remained to save enough money that they could eventually retire in China, where the cost of living was lower. But given that most Chinese had only menial jobs, it is doubtful that many could have realized their dream. Many Chinese men in Canada lost contact with their families during the Second World War when Japan invaded China. The dream of reunion became even more distant after the war, when the Communist Party of China defeated the Nationalist Party to establish a socialist government: the Sinophobia of the West in the fifties, and the subsequent Cold War between the capitalist and communist worlds, made it virtually impossible for Chinese men in Canada to join their families. Although some were able to sponsor their families from Taiwan and Hong Kong during the fifties and sixties, many had to wait until the seventies, when diplomatic relations between Canada and China were normalized, before family reunion was possible. In 1973, during the visit of Prime Minister Trudeau to China, an agreement was signed to enable relatives of Chinese-Canadians to emigrate from China to Canada. Within one year of the agreement Chinese-Canadians had filed 6,000 applications for immigration visas for about 15,000 relatives, 90 per cent of whom lived in the Guangdong (Kwangtung) province (*Montreal Star* 1974). Not all the applicants, however, were successful. The media reported some of the successful cases in 1974 (*New York Times*, 1974; *Toronto Star*, 1974; *Montreal Star*, 1974). Some of the married bachelors never had a chance to reunite with their families and for those who did, the period of separation was terribly long.[2]

A study of elderly Chinese who came to Canada before 1923 (Li, 1982, 1985) found many examples of forced separation before the repeal of the Chinese Immigration Act in 1947. As one respondent decribed it:

> Everybody was like that. You came here [to Canada] and if you behaved, then you could go home and meet the family again. . . .
> Sometimes you came here for thirty or forty years, fifty or sixty

years, and never went back to see them. . . . I know of one guy
here, when he went back to China to get married, he lived there
for a couple of months. . . . He never saw his wife [again] for forty
years. . . . You came in here . . . year after year, worked a little
bit, spent a little bit, couldn't save money to see your wife. . . .
So what could you do? (Interview transcripts)

In many cases the family did not reunite until years after the
marriage (Hoe, 1976: 271–5; Li, 1980a). Lee, eighty-four in 1980,
described his life as follows:

I came to Canada in 1913. I came from Taishan. . . . When I came,
I was seventeen years old. It was very hard. I was young and no
one came with me. I had no money then. . . . I got married in
1919. . . . I went back to China. . . . My parents matched us. I
was back for one year or so. . . . My wife came when she was
sixty-three years old [1964]. Now [1980] she is seventy-nine. (Ibid.)

Although many married bachelors maintained contact with their
families through remittances and correspondence, many family
members remained strangers because of the long periods of separation (Hoe, 1976). Eng, for example, who met his father, in
Canada, for the first time in 1951, described the meeting as
follows:

I came in 1951. . . . I was nineteen. . . . Before I came, I looked at
the picture [of my father] and I knew what he looked like. . . .
There were three guys sitting in the kitchen, and then I asked my
cousin, 'Which one is my dad?' and he said, 'At the corner, that
one.' And then my dad shook hands with me, that's it. I felt really
funny. (Ibid.)

The long absence of men from home also disrupted the social
lives of their families. Frequently the remittances they sent home
became the families' sole source of financial support. As Eng
explained:

We depended on Dad to send money to support us. We didn't
have a man old enough to farm, so we had to hire someone to do
the farming for us. . . . At the end of the year, we did the harvest,
and sold the rice, and then paid the guy that we hired. . . . My
dad was not rich but he was the kind of guy that really looked
after the family. I know that he earned about $140 a month and
every time he sent $100 back to support us, he only had $40 for
all kinds of expenses. (Ibid.)

When the remittances were cut off during the Second World War, many families experienced economic hardship and even starvation. A Chinese woman who came to Canada in 1958 described her tragedy:

> During the starvation, there was nothing to eat. . . . We went to pick the pea leaves, and boiled them [for food] . . . Back home at that time, it was very hard, the people had nothing to eat and they died, starved to death. . . . At that time, my husband could not send money back. . . . He sent me money but it did not reach me . . . . In 1958 I came, on Christmas Day. I came for one year and then my husband died. (Ibid.)

Aside from the hardship of being separated from their husbands, many wives in China had to raise their children by themselves. When the sons reached their teens some joined their fathers overseas. An elderly Chinese woman recounted the painful experience of sending her son to her husband shortly after the war:

> He was in his late teens. . . . His father sent a letter and told him to come. . . . I didn't want him to go because he was the only son. . . . My mother-in-law and I both didn't want him to leave. So I had to explain to her because she didn't understand. . . . I told her that it would be good for his future and so she let him go. If he stayed at home, there was no work for him to do. . . . My son was gone for a long time before I came. (Ibid.)

Table 4.3 provides further evidence about the married life in separation among the Chinese in Canada. The 1941 data indicate that of the 29,033 Chinese men in Canada 23,556, or over 80 per cent, were married. In contrast, only 1,177, or 50 per cent, of the Chinese women were married. These statistics produce a sex ratio of 2,001 married men to 100 married women and give further credence to the pattern of married life in separation before the war. Although it is theoretically possible for some Chinese to have married members of other ethnic groups, inter-ethnic marriages were rare because of social discrimination (Hoe, 1976: 267; Woodsworth, 1941: 144).[3] Despite an improvement in gender imbalance in the post-war census years, the ratio remained high. In 1951 there were 17,155 married Chinese men to 2,842 married Chinese women: a sex ratio of 604 to 100. In 1961 the ratio was 18,013 married men to 11,275 married women, or 160 to 100.

TABLE 4.3

MARITAL STATUS BY SEX, FOR CHINESE IN CANADA
15 YEARS OF AGE AND OVER, 1941–71

Marital Status	1941		1951		1961		1971	
	N	%	N	%	N	%	N	%
Male								
Single	4,186	14.4	4,739	20.7	7,398	27.5	15,610	35.6
Married	23,556	81.1	17,155	75.1	18,013	67.0	26,285	59.9
Widowed or divorced	1,291	4.4	954	4.2	1,458	5.4	1,975	4.5
Total	29,033	99.9	22,848	100.0	26,869	99.9	43,870	100.0
Female								
Single	992	42.4	1,455	31.8	2,019	14.2	9,390	24.6
Married	1,177	50.4	2,842	62.1	11,275	79.4	24,350	63.7
Widowed or divorced	168	7.2	281	6.1	906	6.4	4,460	11.7
Total	2,337	100.0	4,578	100.0	14,200	100.0	38,200	100.0
Males per 100 females								
Single	422		326		366		166	
Married	2,001		604		160		108	
Widowed or divorced	769			340	161		44	
Total	1,242		499		189		115	

SOURCES: Compiled from Censuses of Canada: 1941, vol. I, table 37, pp. 698–9; 1951, vol. II, table 31, pp. 31:1–31:2; 1961, vol. I, part 3, bulletin 1.3–7, table 106, pp. 106:1–106:12; 1971, vol. I, part 4, bulletin 1.4–6, table 14.

Table 4.4 shows estimates of the number of intact and broken families among the Chinese from 1941 to 1971. The number of intact conjugal families more than doubled from 1,177 in 1941 to 2,842 in 1951. It further increased to 11,275 in 1961, and 24,350 in 1971, as the sex ratio of new immigrants after the war was approaching a balance. For example, between 1947 and 1962 the ratio of Chinese entering Canada was 98 men to 100 women; and between 1963 and 1967, 72 men to 100 women (Li, 1980a: 62). These changes reflect the family reunification after the war and the increasing number of family immigrations as a result of less restrictive immigration policies. Table 4.4 also shows correspond-

TABLE 4.4

ESTIMATED NUMBERS OF FAMILY TYPES AMONG CHINESE IN CANADA, 1941–71

Family type	1941	1951	1961	1971
Intact conjugal family[a]	1,177	2,842	11,275	24,350
'Broken' family				
(a) Divorced or widowed[b]	1,459	1,235	2,364	6,435
(b) 'Separated', wife outside of Canada[c]	20,141	12,882	5,384	1,558

SOURCE: Table 4.3
[a] Assumes monogamy and no inter-ethnic marriages among Chinese women. The figures are based on the number of Chinese women reported married. This may slightly overestimate the number of intact families, given the theoretical possibility of some Chinese women marrying men of other ethnic origins.
[b] Figures based on the number of Chinese males and females reported divorced or widowed.
[c] For 1941 and 1951 the estimate assumes a maximum of 20% and a minimum of 0% inter-ethnic marriages among Chinese males. The maximum is based on the estimate of 20.1% inter-ethnic marriages among 'Asiatic' in 1961, and 19.5% in 1971, censuses of Canada. (See Ramu, 1976: table 7, p. 332.) The actual calculation for 1941 and 1951 assumes an average of 10% inter-ethnic marriages. For 1941, for example, the number of married male Chinese (23,556) − the number of married female Chinese (1,177) × .9 = the number of married men, wife outside of Canada (20,141). For 1961, 20.1% inter-ethnic marriages are assumed; and for 1971, 19.5%. Given the likelihood of overestimation for other categories in the table, this category is a conservative estimate.

ingly that 'separated' families declined in number from 20,141 in 1941 to 12,882 in 1951, and 5,384 in 1961. By 1971 the family patterns were almost the reverse of those in 1941. These trends clearly show the prevalence of married life in separation among the Chinese before the war. They also indicate the effects of immigration policies on the Chinese family structure in the post-war years.

The delay of a second generation

The absence of Chinese women had further implications for the Chinese community in Canada. Among other things, it inhibited the growth of a second generation of Chinese-Canadians. Table 4.2 shows that the number of native-born Chinese-Canadians increased slowly from 7 per cent in 1921 to 12 per cent in 1931, to 20 per cent in 1941. The post-war immigration pattern brought the native-born population to 31 per cent in 1951, to 40 per cent in 1961, and 38 per cent in 1971. Despite these increases, 75 per cent of the Chinese in Canada remained foreign-born as late as 1981, 123 years after the arrival of the first Chinese in Canada. Undoubtedly this delay of the second generation can be partly attributed to the policy of exclusion before the war, and partly to a larger volume of immigration after it, which increased the foreign-born component of the Chinese population in Canada. In contrast, the native-born population among Japanese adults in the Canadian labour force in 1971 was 76 per cent, as compared with 20 per cent among the Chinese (Li, 1980b). This dramatic difference was largely due to the Canadian immigration policy towards the Japanese, which had permitted them to bring their wives to Canada since 1908 (see Adachi, 1976).

The magnitude of the foreign-born population is more dramatic among the Chinese adult population. In 1981, for example, 86 per cent of the employed Chinese in the Canadian labour market, 15 years of age and over, were foreign-born (Census of Canada, 1981). Undoubtedly the large proportion of foreign-born among the Chinese had a further impact on their occupational and other achievements, given the importance of family background and nativity on the career cycle (Jencks, 1972; Boyd, et al., 1985). The absence of a sizeable native-born population also explains why the Chinese had relatively little political influence in Canada (Li, 1987).

The family and labour reproduction

The foregoing analysis shows how the Chinese-Canadian family was constrained by the Canadian exclusionary policy before 1947, with the end result that many married men were forced to live apart from their wives and children. In so doing they answered the needs of capitalist expansion in Canada in several ways.

The Chinese came to Canada as an inferior labour group to perform the menial jobs that employers found difficult to fill with white workers. Because of poverty and destitution at home they were forced to accept highly undesirable conditions in order to work in Canada. They had to pay a head tax to enter the country, and then to engage in jobs that paid less than those available to white workers; they came in their prime working age and left their families behind. From the point of view of capitalists and employers, the procurement of Chinese workers was an effective means of what some authors (Bolaria and Li, 1985: 187) call 'inter-nationalizing the labour reserve'. In addition to providing the benefits of cheap labour immediately, recruitment from outside the country meant that the state did not have to pay the cost of producing this labour. That cost, in terms of at least raising those workers to prime working age, had already been borne by the country from which they were recruited. In other words, the poor countries of the world provided the capitalist countries with cheap labour that was ready-made, available to be absorbed whenever it was needed.

Once the initial flow of labour was secured, the basic problem was how to maintain the reproduction of easily manageable labour at a low cost so that the menial jobs in the capitalist system could continue to be performed efficiently. The reproduction of labour involves the cost of replenishing the labour power of workers; aside from the basic costs of food and shelter, it means financing the infrastructures for maintaining a work force. Such infrastructures may include the worker's family, which provides emotional and other support in addition to reproducing another generation of workers, and other institutions such as schools and hospitals for the proper upkeep of a healthy labour force. It can easily be seen that if workers recruited from outside the country left their families behind, the cost of labour reproduction would be lower. The state would not be responsible for maintaining those families; that cost would then be borne by the workers themselves through the remittances they sent home. In addition to bearing the financial cost of supporting their families, the individual workers, as in the case of the Chinese, also had to pay the emotional cost of separation. The isolation in turn tended to produce a transient mentality, in which they often docilely accepted harsh working conditions and hostile social treatment, as they looked on their stay as a sojourn, a temporary situation.

This argument is consistent with the experiences of the Chinese in Canada. Using their low earnings to support both themselves and their families in China, many were compelled to maintain an extremely frugal standard of living—one that white workers often considered to be below subsistence. It was on this ground that white workers accused the Chinese of engaging in unfair competition because they would accept a lower wage (Royal Commissions, 1885, 1902). In this way Chinese workers not only provided cheap labour for industrial development but also helped to weaken working-class solidarity, by diverting potential class conflicts to racial antagonism.

In most cases the children of the Chinese married bachelors were raised in China, where the standard of living was lower. When these children, especially sons, grew to working age they often followed in their fathers' footsteps and sought work in Canada. Thus the family in separation helped the Canadian state to reproduce another generation of cheap labour without having to bear the overhead cost. At the same time, generations of Chinese workers were kept permanently to a foreign status, which forced them to be marginal in Canadian society and made it difficult for them to be upwardly mobile.

5

Community Organizations
and Social Life

Throughout the history of the Chinese in Canada, many types of community organizations were formed. The basic purpose of these associations was to resolve the community's internal problems and to deal with the external pressures of discrimination and segregation. A number of factors contributed to their development. Racism and discrimination by white society posed an external threat and produced a certain degree of internal solidarity in response to outside pressures. As a result of legislative controls and social hostilities, the Chinese were excluded from participating in many social institutions of white Canadians; by the turn of the century it is evident that they were subjected to severe economic, residential, educational, and social segregation. The Chinese associations provided some alternatives to blocked opportunities in Canadian society.

Many associations developed a quasi-judiciary system for adjudicating internal disputes (Lyman, Willmott, and Ho, 1964; Willmott, 1964). Although the Chinese were not excluded from Canadian courts, two factors probably explain why they preferred to settle disputes internally through community associations: the inability of many to speak English and their apprehension that they would not receive a just hearing in Canadian courts. Such apprehension was well-founded given the attitude of Canadian law-enforcement agencies towards the Chinese. The Honourable Mr. N.W.T. Drake, President of the Council, British Columbia, made the following statement before the 1885 Royal Commission:

> The Chinese are utterly unacquainted with truth, and it is a universal comment on their evidence that you cannot believe anything they say. They shelter themselves under their ignorance of the English language so that no cross-examination can reach them, and it is generally believed that the interpreters guide the evidence. (Royal Commission, 1885: 154)

This kind of bias was widely shared among law-enforcement officers (Royal Commission, 1885: 213).

The voluntary organizations also provided mutual aid and social services to the sojourners, especially in times of need. For example, many associations set up hostels for Chinese who needed a temporary place to stay (Lyman, Willmott, and Ho, 1964). When the Victoria public-school system attempted to seg-regate the Chinese from other students, the Chinese associations built separate schools for the Chinese to boycott the public schools (Ashworth, 1979: 77; Lee, 1967: 357-8). Undoubtedly the absence of their wives and children increased the Chinese men's reliance on community associations for emotional and material support. In such conditions it is easy to understand why the various Chinese associations were so popular in the nineteenth century and the first half of the twentieth. Their decline in recent decades has largely reflected the different needs of the post-war immigrants.

The way in which the Chinese formed associations in Canada showed ingenious use of limited resources for mobilizing collec-tive efforts. Since most of the Chinese who immigrated in the nineteenth century were working-class men, they were limited in the organizational skills and finances they could devote to developing community organizations. Aside from the external factors, such as institutional racism and legal exclusion, that cre-ated the need to unite, a number of internal factors and back-ground characteristics probably made it easier for the Chinese to form various associations. Since those who came to Canada in the nineteenth century emigrated predominantly from a small number of counties in southeastern China (Lai, 1975), common locality provided a basis for social organization. Districts of origin often meant not only differences of allegiance or identity, but also substantial variations in dialects. Unlike the Chinese in Southeast Asia, where five or more languages were used, those in Canada were culturally and linguistically quite homogeneous (Willmott, 1970). Moreover, common surnames, or clans, ena-bled them to use both real and pseudo-kinship for social orga-nization. Although clans in China had the limited function of defining exogamy, clanship-based associations in Canada per-formed many functions (Willmott, 1964).[1] However, as Willmott notes, a distinction should be made between clans in China and clan associations in Canada. The latter included only Chinese of the same surname, and not all resident members of the clan. Thus the clan associations operated more on a basis of institutionalized friendship than of clanship (Chow, 1976). Another principle of community organization was to model these associations after the secret societies in China, which had played an important part in local organizations (Willmott, 1970).

The emergence of Chinese social organizations

In fact, the first organizations formed by the Chinese in Canada were neither clan associations nor locality or district associations, but fraternal associations that had their origin in the secret societies of China (Willmott, 1964). According to available historical documents, the first such society in Canada, a chapter of the Zhi Gong Tang (Chih-kung T'ang), was founded in Barkerville, B.C., in 1862 (Lyman, Willmott and Ho, 1964). Later chapters were formed in other gold-mining towns such as Quesnel Mouth, in 1876, and Yale, in 1882 (Con, et al., 1982: 34). A rival branch of the Hong Society (Hung-men) was formed in Victoria in 1897 (Lyman, 1970: 48), and there are indications that by 1903 the order of secret societies had local, regional, and provincial divisions (Lyman, Willmott and Ho, 1964).

The Zhi Gong Tang,[2] also known as Hongmen (Hung-men) had its origins in the Triad Society, believed to have been established in China by the early eighteenth century. Its purpose was to overthrow the Qing (Ch'ing) Dynasty, which ruled from 1644 to 1911, and to restore the Ming Dynasty (1368–1644). Between 1787 and 1911, chapters of the Triad Society participated in a number of insurgencies against the Qing (Ch'ing) Dynasty (Lyman, 1970). There were five branches of the Hongmen supposedly tracing back to the five monks who were believed to have founded the Society. These branches operated in different provinces of China, each with its own local chapters (Lee, 1967: 228–9). Often the local chapters functioned autonomously and served as useful instruments of grievance for the populace (Lyman, 1970: 39). According to the insignia of the Hong leagues (Hung-men) in Canada, it seems that they originated from the second branch of the Hong Society in China, which flourished in the Pearl River Delta of Guangdong (Kwangtung) province during the middle of the nineteenth century (Lee, 1967: 230).

It appears that chapters of the Chinese secret societies in Canada were more concerned with local affairs affecting daily life than with politics in China, although there were times where political changes in China prompted actions from these overseas organizations.[3] According to a set of original rules and regulations of the Zhi Gong Tang written shortly after 1882, and discovered in 1961 by a park ranger in Barkerville, the purpose in forming the society was 'to maintain a friendly relationship' among the people from China and 'to accumulate wealth through proper business methods for the benefit of all members' (Lyman, 1970: 51).[4] The activities of the Society extended from running a hostel for Chinese to arbitrating disputes. One regulation states:

> Any quarrel and dispute among members may be referred to the T'ang, which will call a meeting to settle the dispute. The member losing the case will be fined one dollar. If he fails to pay the fine immediately, he will be sentenced to six stripes. Sentence will be decided by the senior members, who will judge the severity of the error committed. Sentence will be carried out in the T'ang. (Lyman, 1970: 55)

Chinese who lived in other towns but required the officers of the Society to arbitrate had to pay their travelling expenses. The rules also indicate that the Society was involved in mutual aid; according to one regulation:

> All the money received by the T'ang is for conducting T'ang affairs. However, those members who are old or sick, or who have suffered disaster caused either by natural calamities or by accidents, and who have no means nor anyone to look after them, may receive care from the T'ang. (Lyman, 1970: 55)

Members who were newly arrived and had no place to stay were offered accommodation and two meals. In addition, the Society set up rules for regulating the livelihood of Chinese miners and workers; members had to respect the policy of 'first come, first served when selling or buying businesses or mines' (Lyman, 1970: 54). They were also prohibited from undercutting each other's wages to compete for jobs. Any members who discovered a good mine were limited to claims of no more than 100 feet for each person (Lyman, 1970: 55). These rules clearly outline an organizational structure on the part of the Zhi Gong Tang that played an important part in the lives of working-class Chinese in mining towns before the turn of the century.

The Chinese Consolidated Benevolent Association

The first community-based Chinese organization[5] was formed in 1884, in Victoria, under the name of the Chinese Consolidated Benevolent Association.[6] Unlike the clan or locality associations, which appealed to members on the basis of a common surname or home county, this one was formed as an umbrella organization purporting to represent the Chinese community as a whole. Prior to its formation the Chinese in Canada had to ask the Consul-General in San Francisco to represent them in dealing with the provincial and Dominion governments of Canada (Lai, 1975). Before the Chinese Consulate was set up in Ottawa in 1908, representatives of the Chinese Consolidated Benevolent Association served as quasi-official spokesmen for the Chinese community on many occasions.

In March, 1884, the Chinese merchants of Victoria sent a letter to the Chinese Consul-General in San Francisco requesting permission to form a Chinese association. The letter described the plight of the Chinese as a result of the discriminatory laws and their oppression by white Canadians. It also pointed out the need to control prostitution, gambling, and fighting in the community that were caused in part by Chinese gangs. Accordingly, the best solution was to form a Chinese association and a Chinese consulate in Victoria (Lee, 1967: 177–8; Lai, 1975). With about $30,000 raised among the Chinese, a building was constructed in 1885.

According to the 1884 Rules and Bylaws of the Chinese Consolidated Benevolent Association, the organization was to provide social services and aid, to resolve disputes, and to fight against oppression from the outside (Lee, 1967: 179–86; Lai, 1975). The rules also indicate that the Association would help Chinese to fight in court against abuses or unfair treatments by white Canadians. These by-laws suggest that racial disputes were frequent, and that the Chinese probably shied away from court proceedings for fear of unfavourable treatment in the Canadian judiciary system. The activities of the Association in the early period can be grouped in four categories, according to Lai (1975): fund-raising for fighting against the discriminatory laws in courts; arbitration of disputes and maintenance of order in Chinatown; raising relief funds for Chinese communities elsewhere; and operating a hospital, a cemetery, and a school.

Although the Chinese Benevolent Association claimed to represent all Chinese in Canada, it was in fact controlled by a small number of merchants,[7] since it had been formed on the initiative of merchants. The by-laws stipulated that the executive positions were to be filled by wealthy Chinese of good reputation (Sedgwick and Willmott, 1974; Lee, 1967: 180). The merchants also provided the most financial support when the association raised money to build a hall (Lee, 1967: 187). Since the officers were mainly merchants, they were chiefly concerned with protecting their own interests (Lai, 1975). When a Chinese shop was burglarized in 1894, for example, the Association put up a large reward for anyone who could provide information leading to an arrest. But the Association did not intervene to assist a Chinese sailor who was assaulted by a white sailor in 1905; later the victim openly denounced the Association for helping the Chinese merchants, but not ordinary Chinese (Lai, 1975). These instances give credence to the claim that the Association often acted in the interests of the small number of Chinese élites.

The proliferation of Chinese organizations and their politics

By the middle of the 1880s there was an established Chinese community in Vancouver. Formed in 1895, the city's Chinese Consolidated Benevolent Association was officially initiated in 1906 (Lee, 1967: 195). Earlier, around 1892, another Chinese Consolidated Benevolent Association had been formed in New Westminster (Lee, 1967: 198).

In addition to the community and fraternal associations, there were many locality associations, based on common county origins. In 1886 the Chinese from Poonyue county established a Victoria branch of their association, which had its headquarters in San Francisco; in 1893 the Chinese from San-ning (Taishan after 1911) formed an association in Victoria (Con, et al., 1982: 40); and by 1898 there were at least ten locality or district associations in Vancouver.

By the time the Chinese Immigration Act of 1923 was enacted about 40 per cent of the Chinese in Canada lived outside British Columbia (see Table 3.3). With the emergence of Chinese communities across Canada came the development of associations in different cities. For example, in 1923 there were ten clan associations and two locality associations in Toronto, while in Calgary there were six clan associations and one locality association

(Wickberg, 1979: 92). At that time Vancouver had twenty-six clan associations and twelve locality associations. By 1937 the clan associations in Vancouver had increased to forty-six and the locality associations to seventeen (Wickberg, 1979: 93). There were corresponding increases in the number of Chinese associations in Toronto and Calgary.

Like the Hongmen (Hung-men) and the Chinese Consolidated Benevolent Association, the clan associations were initially formed to help their members. Their activities included arbitrating disputes and providing social, economic, and at times legal services to members (Willmott, 1964).

Although the Chinese associations were mainly involved in matters affecting the daily life of the Chinese in Canada, on a number of occasions political developments in China created divisions among them. Towards the end of the nineteenth century China faced both the internal problems of poverty and overpopulation and the external pressures of foreign domination. As China was defeated by one foreign power after another, it became increasingly evident to Chinese patriots and intellectuals that political changes were inevitable.

Two political movements emerged from this period. On the one hand was the reform movement led by Kang Youwei (K'ang Yu-wei) to modernize China within the framework provided by an enlightened emperor. On the other was the revolutionary force led by Sun Yat-sen, who deemed the Qing (Ch'ing) government hopeless and sought to overthrow it. Kang visited Canada in 1899 after his reform attempt with the Emperor was smashed by Empress Dowager Cixi (Tz'u-hsi).[8] During his visit he established a China Reform Association in Victoria to advocate his political cause of reform in China. In one of the organizing meetings a local Chinese leader suggested changing the name in Chinese to the Society to Save the Emperor, with the purpose of counteracting the conservative forces of the Empress Dowager (Lo, 1967: 180).

Within five or six years there were eleven branches of the China Reform Association in different parts of Canada (Lee, 1967: 289). The Association received its major support from prosperous Chinese merchants and leaders of clan associations in Canada (Lee, 1967: 289). In the few years after 1899 it also had the support of the Zhi Gong Tang (Chih-kung T'ang). But after 1905 the Zhi Gong Tang allied with the Tongmeng Hui (T'ung-meng Hui) or

United League, which Sun Yat-sen had set up in Victoria and Vancouver during his visits to Canada (Lee, 1967). Sun visited Canada in 1897 and 1911, and these visits were greatly facilitated by the Zhi Gong Tang, which provided a forum for Sun's revolutionary cause (Wickberg, 1980). By the time he visited Canada in 1911 the Zhi Gong Tang and the Tongmeng Hui were cooperating very well with each other.

The Chinese in Canada also provided considerable financial support to a number of uprisings in China, which led to the eventual overthrow of the Qing government in October, 1911. After 1911 the Zhi Gong Tang split with the United League, now called the Chinese Nationalist League, and operated as a branch of the Guomindang (Kuomintang) or Nationalist party in China. Between 1911 and 1919 the Zhi Gong Tang and the Chinese Nationalist League competed along with other clan and locality associations for control of the Chinese Benevolent Association (Wickberg, 1980). The competition was caused in part by differences in political ideologies and allegiances originating in China.

There were rare occasions too when political developments in Canada or China changed the alliance of the Chinese associations and bonded them together to form a united front, if only temporarily. One such was the advent of the Chinese Immigration Act of 1923. A national federation of Chinese organizations, called the Chinese Association of Canada, was established in Toronto to fight the bill (Wickberg, 1980). In Vancouver the Chinese associations also formed joint committees and launched fund-raising efforts to oppose it. A number of Chinese unions, such as the Chinese Shingle Workers Federation and the Chinese Produce Sellers Group, issued joint statements arguing for a modification of the bill (Wickberg, 1980). Although these efforts brought unity to the Chinese associations, they were of no avail in stopping the Chinese Immigration Act from becoming law.

Another demonstration of unity was prompted by the outbreak of the Sino-Japanese war in 1937, when Japan invaded China. To raise money for the war, the Chinese government issued a war bond and asked the overseas Chinese to support it. In response to that appeal the Chinese in Canada formed the Chinese Liberty Fund Association to promote the bonds, and in Victoria alone $69,000 were raised within sixteen months between 1938 and 1939. In total, 23 Chinese associations and

2,579 Chinese individuals purchased these bonds in Victoria (Lai, 1980).

Social life and vice activities in Chinatowns

In many cities throughout North America it is common to find a number of blocks, near the downtown area, known as Chinatown. The Chinatowns today are mainly commercial and tourist districts where many Chinese businesses operate. In the nineteenth century, however, the Chinatown was both a commercial area and a community centre. Chinese businesses drew their customers from the Chinese residents of the quarter and from a transient population of Chinese miners and labourers from remote areas. In many respects the Chinatowns were ethnic ghettos. Living conditions were unsanitary and overcrowded, and there were violent crimes such as murder and kidnapping (Lee, 1967: 104–9; Lai, 1972: 58). Besides the legitimate businesses, vice activities including gambling, opium-smoking, and prostitution could be found in the Chinatowns. As more Chinese settled in Victoria, New Westminster, and later Vancouver, Chinatowns developed in these communities. Earlier, in the mining period, many Chinese had also settled in the mining communities of British Columbia and set up areas characterized by Chinese shops and residential buildings (Lee, 1967: 81–5). By the 1880s the most developed Chinatown was in Victoria, which had about two thousand Chinese and over a hundred Chinese stores (Lee, 1967: 91). There were also fifteen opium dens, eleven hotels serving the Chinese, and three companies playing Chinese opera (Con, et al., 1982: 36).

Like other ethnic settlements in urban Canada, the Chinatown in Victoria began with a few shops where some Chinese businesses operated. Its growth was directly related to an increase in the Chinese population; by 1881 the Chinese accounted for about one-third of Victoria's 6,000 people (Lee, 1967: 81), providing the population base for the Chinese community to develop.

Undoubtedly anti-orientalism and institutional exclusion prevented the Chinese from being accepted in many white communities. The Chinatown served as a segregated area where the Chinese lived and carried out their business transactions.

Although the majority of Chinese were labourers, a class structure was evident in these early Chinese communities in urban
Canada. At the top of the community was an élite made up
exclusively of Chinese merchants. The rest of the Chinatown
was composed of working-class Chinese, including a transient
population of miners and labourers who used the Chinatown as
a base whenever they were not employed. The Chinese merchants controlled the trading companies and formed neighbour-
hood associations to promote their influence in the community
(Con, et al., 1982: 35-6). Some of the firms were involved in
recruiting Chinese workers for white employers (Lee, 1967: 126-
8). The trading companies also sent remittances and letters to
China on behalf of the Chinese workers (Con, et al., 1982: 35).
There is evidence to suggest that some of the merchants were
involved in the opium trade and operating opium factories (Royal
Commission, 1902: 15).

In discussing the poor living conditions and vice activities in
the Chinatowns of Victoria and Vancouver, the 1902 Royal Commission noted important differences in how the merchant class
and labourers lived. For example, the commissioners described
their visit to a Chinese merchant's home as follows:

> We were admitted into that gentleman's private apartments, con-
> sisting of four rooms well furnished after the Oriental style. Here
> we were introduced to his family, consisting of wife and three
> small children. The surroundings here were sufficiently neat and
> orderly to satisfy even the most fastidious taste. (Royal Commis-
> sion, 1902: 15)

The way the Chinese merchants lived was in sharp contrast to
the living conditions of the Chinese workers. Describing a board-
ing house occupied by the better class of Chinese labourers in
the Victoria Chinatown, the commissioners wrote:

> Ascending a narrow stairway we enter what had apparently once
> been a large room, some 18 × 30 feet, with a 10 foot ceiling, but
> which had an additional floor, occupying a position nearly mid-
> way between the floor and the ceiling, thus making two stories
> out of one. The lower floor was divided off into small rooms
> reached by a number of narrow hallways, each room containing
> three low bunks covered with a Chinese mat. In many cases a
> double tier of these bunks was observed. . . . The second or upper
> floor was reached by a short stairway. Here no attempt seems to

have been made at a division of space. . . . In many cases even a third floor exists, reached usually by a narrow ricketty stairway, into which the occupant crawls upon his hands and knees. Here we found an almost entire absence of light and ventilation, the occupants using a small smoky, open lamp, to discover their respective locations, the fumes from which add to the discomfort of the surroundings. (Ibid.)

The commissioners described even worse living conditions for the 'common coolie':

Entering a long, dark, narrow alleyway, our guide leading the way by striking a match at intervals, stumbling along over a muddy, uneven walk, the faint glimmer of a light appears in the distance . . . revealing a net-work of small, partly covered passageways leading in all directions through this human beehive. . . . Three low bunks surround the room (often a double tier of them). . . . The walls are blackened with smoke. . . . The walls and floor, which was composed of rough lumber, are absolutely bare, and the starry heavens are observable at intervals through the roof. . . . Here again we found an entire absence of any attempt at ventilation. . . . The atmosphere of the room is fairly stifling. (Ibid.: 15–16)

Given the conditions the Chinese workers lived in and the types of jobs they held, the sense of social isolation must have been immense in the absence of the family. This largely explains the popularity of opium-smoking and gambling among the Chinese workers seeking some temporary relief.[9] The vice activities in Chinatown were also the main sources of social interaction for these lone workers, since racial and class barriers prevented them from participating in white communities. This point was well explained by an elderly Chinese:

There was no family, everyone was single. What were you going to do after work? Where would you go? . . . If you went to the gambling house, you could talk and laugh. Some went to win money, others went to learn the latest news, or just to watch. So that's where we went. Where else could we go? (Interview transcripts)

The social and living conditions of the Chinese were viewed by many white Canadians as a public disgrace. The Protestant clergy in particular regarded the Chinese as spreading paganism through their loathsome culture and vices (Ward, 1974). Guided by this view, the Methodists revitalized the mission in Victoria among the Chinese in 1885, and in the 1890s the Anglicans and Presbyterians followed suit (Ward, 1974). These churches organized many activities in Chinatown as a means of Christianizing the Chinese. In the 1880s the Methodist Church opened a home in Victoria to help Chinese prostitutes (Ward, 1974). The churches also provided some social and educational programs for the Chinese; the most popular were the evening English classes, which attracted many thousands of adult Chinese over many years (Ward, 1974).

The social life of the Chinese was largely conditioned by the social and demographic characteristics of their community. The denial of family life increased the need of the lone Chinese to rely on the community for support. The Chinese organizations responded to their needs and used common surnames and home counties as bases for recruiting members. The vice industries capitalized on the problems of the Chinese male society by offering emotional escape to the married bachelors separated from their wives. The restrictive immigration law in Canada prolonged this imbalanced demographic condition until many years after the Second World War. Excluding Chinese from entering Canada since 1923 had an evident effect on the demographic structure of the Chinese community. For example, by 1937-38 nearly 95 per cent of the Chinese in Victoria were male, and about half were between 50 and 69 years of age (Lai, 1980: 14). As late as the 1960s there was a conspicuous absence of Chinese leaders among the first-generation immigrants aged 35 to 50 (Willmott, 1964: 35). It took many years after the war to correct these conditions. As the post-war Chinese immigrants entered Canada in larger volume they gradually altered the structure of the Chinese community. Correspondingly, the importance of the Chinese associations and vice activities declined as they failed to meet the needs of the post-war immigrants.

III

THE EMERGENCE OF THE CHINESE COMMUNITY AFTER THE WAR

6

Chinese Immigration to Canada

Historically, the development of the Chinese community in Canada was restricted by the Canadian immigration policy and anti-Chinese laws. Legislative controls on immigration produced a definite effect on the size of Chinese population and the structure of the Chinese community in Canada. In 1881 the Chinese population in Canada stood at 4,383 (see Table 4.2): by 1891 it had increased to 9,129. It is difficult to assess the effect of the $50 head tax, required after 1885, on the inflow of Chinese immigrants, who apparently continued to come to Canada in spite of it. Between 1891 and 1901 the Chinese population in Canada almost doubled, from 9,129 to 17,312, and in the next ten years it increased to 27,831. Although the head tax, which was raised to $100 in 1900 and $500 in 1903, did not reduce the number of Chinese entering Canada, it did slow down the rate of increase. Nevertheless, the number of Chinese continued to rise in every census year until after 1931, when it began to decline. Undoubtedly this drop was brought about by the Chinese Immigration Act of 1923, which totally excluded the Chinese from entering Canada. The restricted opportunities in Canada for Chinese also prompted some of them to return to China. As a result the Chinese population in Canada shrank about 12,000 from 46,519 in 1931 to 34,627 in 1941, and it continued to decline slowly from 1941 to 1951. It was not until the post-war years, when the restrictive immigration policy towards the Chinese was replaced by a more favourable one, that the Chinese population again began to show signs of increase. By 1961 it had risen to 58,197. Further changes in the immigration act in 1967 permitted Chinese to be admitted, for the first time in history, under the same criteria as other immigrants. Consequently the Chinese population increased to 118,815 in 1971, and between 1971 and 1981 it doubled again to 289,245.

Compared to their treatment before the war, the situation for the Chinese in Canada after it was a great improvement. Many discriminatory laws were rescinded and their civil rights were gradually recognized. Parliament repealed the Chinese Immigration Act in 1947, lifting a barrier that had lasted for twenty-four years. The Chinese in British Columbia were allowed to vote in 1947, and those in Saskatchewan in 1951. By the late fifties most of the discriminatory clauses against the Chinese had been removed from provincial and federal statutes.

The enfranchisement of the Chinese

A number of factors helped the Chinese to gain suffrage after the war. Two years after the founding of the Cooperative Commonwealth Federation, in 1932, the party advocated the enfranchisement of orientals in the Canadian House of Commons (Lee, 1976). However, the CCF's position on the oriental question was ambiguous. On the one hand, the party advocated granting equal rights to orientals who were native-born or naturalized Canadians; on the other, it supported a restriction on oriental immigration, and during the war it endorsed the evacuation of Japanese from the west coast (MacInnis and MacInnis, undated).[1] Prior to 1947 the CCF had raised the question of enfranchising the orientals several times, but their efforts did not succeed. The party suffered a setback in the 1935 federal election in B.C., where the Liberals equated a vote for the CCF with a vote to grant the Chinese and Japanese voting rights (Lee, 1976). However, the CCF position on the Chinese and Japanese opened a political issue that eventually led to their enfranchisement.

When Japan invaded China in 1937 popular sentiment in Canada was against Japan in support of China. Shortly after, the Canadian government was concerned with whether Japanese-Canadians on the west coast posed a threat to the internal security of the country (Sunahara, 1981). Ironically, the public image of the Chinese was enhanced as a result of resentment towards the Japanese. When the Special Committee on Orientals in B.C. was appointed on October 1, 1940, to investigate the position of Japanese and Chinese, it considered the problem of the Chinese to be neither difficult nor urgent. Consequently, the report focused exclusively on the Japanese (Special Committee on Orientals in B.C., 1940). After the attack on Pearl Harbor in December, 1941, Canada declared war on Japan and became an ally of China. In 1942 the Government of Canada began its forced evacuation of the Japanese in B.C. beyond the Rocky Mountains, interning them in interior camps. Once again, the public hostility towards the orientals was absorbed by the Japanese-Canadians.

The Chinese meanwhile enjoyed an improved image as many made important contributions during the war, volunteering service overseas, joining the Red Cross, and participating in loan drives for the war effort. (Lee, 1976); the Chinese community oversubscribed every Victory Loan Drive, and in Vancouver contributed more per person than any other group in Canada (Lee, 1976). When China emerged after the war as one of the victors over Japan, it became embarrassing for Canada to maintain a discriminatory policy towards a racial group of an allied country, especially when the policy contradicted the statements on human rights embodied in the charter of the United Nations. Earlier, in 1943, the United States had repealed its Chinese Exclusion Act and allowed a quota of 105 Chinese to be admitted annually (Li, 1977). In 1945, a year after the Dominion government had enlisted Chinese-Canadians in British Columbia for compulsory military training, the British Columbia government made concessions on the issue of oriental franchise by granting the right to vote to oriental soldiers in the Canadian Armed Forces (Lee, 1976). The enactment of the Canadian Citizenship Act in 1946 also made it more difficult for Canada to maintain a second-class citizenship status for orientals. A year later the franchise was extended to civilian Chinese-Canadians as well (Lee, 1976). In the same year Parliament repealed the Chinese Immigration Act of 1923 (Statutes of Canada 1947, c. 19).

During the long struggle for civil rights the Chinese community across Canada mobilized considerable efforts to oppose legal discrimination. For example, in 1936 several Chinese leaders in Toronto formed the Committee for the Movement to Abolish the Canadian Restrictive Immigration Policy Towards Chinese (Lee, 1967: 369). In 1944, when the Dominion government conscripted Chinese-Canadians for military service, an Anglican clergyman named Law founded the Chinese-Canadian Association in Vancouver to lobby for enfranchisement of the Chinese. The Association collected 700 signatures and presented a brief to the B.C. cabinet in 1945 (Lee, 1976: 56–7). Around the same time the Taishan (T'ai-shan) Association in Vancouver passed a number of resolutions calling for the repeal of the Chinese Immigration

Act (Con, et al., 1982: 205). However, coming from a politically powerless group, these efforts brought little change. It was only through the mediation of political parties and civil-liberties groups that new civil rights were eventually secured (Lee, 1976).

Changes in Canadian immigration policy

Despite the repeal of the Chinese Immigration Act, Chinese immigration to Canada prior to 1962 was highly restricted in comparison with the relatively free migration from Europe and the United States (Li and Bolaria, 1979). After the war the Chinese were placed under the same restrictive conditions of admission as other Asians. These conditions were specified in an order-in-council of 1930 (P.C. 1930–2115),[2] which in fact prohibited 'the landing in Canada of any immigrant of any Asiatic race' except the wife or unmarried children under eighteen years of age of Canadian citizens.[3] This restrictive policy towards Asians was maintained at a time when Canada was broadening admission from Europe and the United States in response to a critical short-age of manpower during the post-war industrial boom (see Green, 1976). In the decade following the war Canada's immi-gration policy was little different from its historical position of favouring immigrants from Europe and the United States, while discouraging immigrants from Asian and other non-white coun-tries (Li and Bolaria, 1979). The policy towards oriental immigra-tion was frankly put by Prime Minister Mackenzie King in the House of Commons on May 1, 1947:

> Large-scale immigration from the orient would change the fun-damental composition of the Canadian population. Any consid-erable oriental immigration would, moreover, be certain to give rise to social and economic problems of a character that might lead to serious difficulties in the field of international relations. The government, therefore, has no thought of making any change in immigration regulations which would have consequences of the kind.
>
> I wish to state quite definitely that, apart from the repeal of the Chinese Immigration Act and the revocation of order in council P.C. 1378 of June 17, 1931, regarding naturalization, the govern-ment has no intention of removing the existing regulations respecting Asiatic immigration unless and until alternative meas-ures of effective control have been worked out. (Canada House of Commons Debates, 1947: 2646)[4]

A subsequent order-in-council passed in 1950, which specified the categories of admissible immigrants to Canada, distinctly stipulated that the provisions for immigration listed in the order-in-council did not apply to 'immigrants of any Asiatic race' (P.C. 1950–2856).

In 1952 the government of Canada passed the Immigration Act, which gave sweeping power to specially designated immigration officers to determine what kinds of people were admissible. However, as a result of a 1956 decision by the Supreme Court of Canada the government was compelled to spell out the precise classes of people to be admitted (Hawkins, 1972: 104). Consequently the categories of admissible immigrants to Canada were specified in an order-in-council on May 24 the same year. Although there was no reference to racial origin as a criterion, the 1956 order-in-council listed the countries from which immigration to Canada was permitted (P.C. 1956–785). Since the Asian countries were not identified, immigrants from these countries were placed in a special class in which only the spouse, unmarried children under twenty-one years of age, and elderly parents of Canadian citizens were admitted (P.C. 1956–785).[5] Later, in explaining this restrictive policy as it applied to the Chinese, J.W. Pickersgill, Minister of Citizenship and Immigration from 1954 to 1957, said:

> The only reason that admission was confined to unmarried children was, of course, that a chain of immigration would have been set up that would have been very hard to control because of the lack of facilities of any kind that could be made available in China to provide accurate information . . . . As I say, in order to make sure, particularly once the communist regime was established in China, that our limited immigration was not permitted to become an avenue for the back door infiltration of communist agents . . . it was felt by the government responsible at that time and has been felt by the present government since that these controls had to be maintained. (House of Commons Debates, June 9, 1960: 4715–16)

Pickersgill also claimed that as a result of the order-in-council (P.C. 1956–785) the admission of immigrants was no longer based on racial origin (House of Commons Debates, June 9, 1960: 4714). Despite this claim, the Department of Citizenship and Immigration continued to use ethnic and racial origins for classifying immigrants in its annual report until 1961; it was only after 1961 that immigrants' countries of origin were used.

The restriction on Chinese immigration to Canada between 1947 and 1962 reflected the racial bias of the Canadian immigration policy against Asian and other non-white immigrants. Although the Chinese Immigration Act of 1923 was repealed in 1947, the Canadian government did not consider Chinese immigrants as equals of European or American immigrants. Since the restrictive measures permitted only the spouses of Chinese-Canadians and their children who were minor and unmarried to be admitted to Canada in the decade after 1947, some Chinese resorted to entering Canada illegally. In some cases children of Chinese-Canadians misrepresented their age to qualify for admission (House of Commons Debates, June 6, 1960). In others, real and fictitious birth certificates indicating a Chinese-Canadian parent were sold to prospective immigrants.[6]

It is difficult to estimate precisely how many Chinese entered Canada through illegal means before 1960. But the question of illegal entry prompted the Canadian government to conduct an investigation in 1959 (Hawkins, 1972: 131-4). On June 9, 1960, Ellen Fairclough, Minister of Citizenship and Immigration, announced that it was not the intention of the government 'to prosecute or deport from the country any Chinese presently in Canada who have not themselves engaged in assisting other Chinese, apart from their own relatives, to enter Canada illegally' (House of Commons Debates, June 9, 1960: 4724). Fairclough also introduced the Chinese Adjustment Statement Program, by which the Chinese who had entered Canada illegally could come forward to make statements about their illegal entry and their true family background, in return for being allowed to remain in Canada if they were of good moral character and had not been systematically engaged in illegal immigration (Hawkins, 1972: 133). Between 1960 and 1970, 11,569 Chinese made use of the program and had their status adjusted (Hawkins, 1972: 133).

In 1962 the government of Canada changed the requirements for immigration by broadening four categories of admission. The first two categories allowed independent immigrants with educational and professional skills to immigrate with their immediate families. The third category was for the immigration of close relatives of Canadian citizens or permanent residents. In these three categories no reference was made to either racial origin or country of origin as an admission requirement. However, the fourth category of admission enabled Canadian citizens or permanent residents to sponsor a wide range of relatives if the person being sponsored was a citizen 'of any country of Europe, including Turkey; or any country of North, Central or South America or adjacent thereto; or of Egypt, Israel or Lebanon' (P.C. 1962–86).[7] Sponsorship of relatives outside these countries was restricted to the 'parent, grandparent, husband, wife or fiancée, or the unmarried son or daughter under twenty-one years of age' of a Canadian citizen or a permanent resident of Canada (P.C. 1962–86). Consequently the Chinese-Canadians were in fact restricted to sponsoring this limited range of relatives. However, as a result of the first two categories of admission, the 1962 order-in-council permitted Chinese who had no relatives in Canada to apply, for the first time since 1923, as independent immigrants (P.C. 1962–86). Further changes in the immigration regulations in 1967 (P.C. 1967–1616) finally resulted in a universal point system that was to be applied to all prospective immigrants, irrespective of country of origin or racial background. Under the point system an immigrant could apply either as an independent or as a nominated relative sponsored by a Canadian citizen or permanent resident. In either case the immigrant would be assessed as well on the basis of his or her education, occupational demand, and age. The point system was further modified on February 24, 1978 (P.C. 1978–486). It took twenty-four years before the Chinese Immigration Act was repealed in 1947, and another twenty years after that before the Canadian immigration law finally recognized a universal standard of assessment to be applied to Chinese and other immigrants.

Between 1979 and 1980 a sizeable group of Chinese came to Canada as refugees. In response to a growing number of refugees in Southeast Asia who had been displaced from Vietnam, Laos, and Kampuchea, in 1978 Canada announced a plan to accept 5,000 Indochinese refugees. After the Geneva Conference of 1979, organized by the United Nations Secretary General to deal with the refugee question, Canada stated that it would accept up to 50,000 Indochinese refugees for resettlement. By April, 1980, it had increased its intake of refugees by 10,000 (Employment and Immigration Canada, 1982). In all, Canada accepted 60,049 Indochinese refugees between 1979 and 1980, about 30 per cent

(18,021) of whom were linguistically Chinese; Cantonese Chinese made up about 20 per cent (12,212) of the total (Employment and Immigration Canada, 1982).

Characteristics of post-war Chinese immigrants

In the two years following the repeal of the Chinese Immigration Act very few Chinese were accepted as immigrants to Canada. Seven Chinese were admitted in 1947, 24 in 1948 (Dept. of Mines and Resources, 1947, 1948), and 111 in 1949 (Dept. of Citizenship and Immigration, 1950). After 1949 the number of Chinese entering Canada increased to 1,036 in 1950, 2,182 in 1951, and 2,745 in 1952 (see Table 6.1). Between 1950 and 1955, 12,449 Chinese immigrated to Canada.

Until 1962 the only category of immigration open to Chinese was that of sponsored relatives of Chinese-Canadians. Many who came in the fifties were wives and children who had been separated from their husbands and fathers during the long period of exclusion. This wave of migration gradually altered the size and structure of the Chinese community in Canada, hitherto characterized by an aging male population. According to the 1951 census there were 32,528 Chinese in Canada, with a sex ratio of 374 men to 100 women (see Table 4.2). As a result of post-war immigration the Chinese community rose to 58,197 by 1961, and the sex ratio was greatly improved: 163 men to 100 women. Table 6.1 shows some of the characteristics of the Chinese immigrants who entered Canada between 1949 and 1955. In 1950 and 1951 the percentages of children and wives immigrating to Canada were exceptionally high. Sixty per cent of the 1,036 Chinese immigrants in 1950 were children and 32 per cent were wives. In 1951, out of the total of 2,182 Chinese immigrants to Canada that year, 60 per cent were children and 25 per cent wives. As more families were reunited the percentage of Chinese children entering Canada gradually declined to 35 per cent of the total Chinese immigrants in 1952, and to 17 per cent in 1955. Between 1949 and 1955, 4,247 Chinese children and 3,325 Chinese wives entered Canada. In contrast, the percentage of Chinese destined for the Canadian labour force in this period was only 21 per cent.

With more changes in immigration laws, new Chinese immigrants began to arrive in Canada, first in limited numbers and then, after 1967, in larger volumes. Migrating in a different his-

TABLE 6.1

CHINESE IMMIGRANTS ADMITTED TO CANADA, 1949–55

Year	Total Chinese Number	%	Destined to labour force %	Not destined to labour force Wives %	Children %	Other[a] %
1949	111	100.0	9.0	69.4	16.2	5.4
1950	1,036	100.1	3.2	31.8	59.6	5.5
1951	2,182	100.0	4.9	25.5	60.4	9.2
1952	2,745	99.9	23.5	20.7	35.3	20.4
1953	1,961	99.9	38.1	22.9	22.7	16.2
1954	1,950	100.0	24.0	31.1	22.1	22.8
1955	2,575	99.9	24.3	28.6	17.4	29.6
Total (1949–55)	12,560		2,639	3,325	4,247	2,349

SOURCES: Compiled from annual reports of Dept. of Mines and Resources, Immigration Branch for the fiscal year ended March 31 (1949); Dept. of Citizenship and Immigration for the fiscal year ended March 31 (1950–53); and Dept. of Citizenship and Immigration for the calendar year ended March 31 (1954–55).
[a]Listed as 'miscellaneous' for 1949–53 and 'other' for 1954–55.

torical period and under different social circumstances, these post-war immigrants were very different from those who came in the early part of the century. Many were urban dwellers from Hong Kong and Taiwan, in contrast to the earlier immigrants from mainly rural backgrounds. Mainland China ceased to be the major source of Chinese immigration to Canada after the 1949 socialist revolution, largely because of the hostile relations between China and the West during the cold war of the 1950s and 1960s.[8] The mainland Chinese who qualified for sponsorship to Canada had to first overcome the legal and political obstacles of immigrating to places like Hong Kong or Taiwan before being able to apply to come to Canada.

Table 6.2 shows the number and the age composition of Chinese immigrating to Canada between 1956 and 1984. In the eleven years between 1956 and 1967, 30,546 Chinese immigrated to Canada. Chinese immigration reached a new high level after

1967 when the new immigration regulations adopted a universal point system to be applied to all groups. In the next eight years, between 1968 and 1976, Canada admitted 90,118 Chinese, about three times the number admitted during the previous period. Between 1977 and 1984, 79,230 Chinese immigrated to Canada. By 1984 a total of 212,374 Chinese had immigrated since the Chinese Immigration Act was repealed in 1947.

TABLE 6.2

AGE COMPOSITION OF CHINESE IMMIGRANTS ADMITTED
TO CANADA, 1956–84

Age group	1956–67 %	1968–76 %	1977–84 %
0–14	22.8	17.7	15.1
15–34	53.1	55.5	45.8
35–54	16.0	15.5	16.9
55 and over	8.0	11.3	22.2
Total	99.9	100.0	100.0
(Number of Chinese)	(30,546)	(90,118)	(79,230)

SOURCES: Compiled from annual reports of Dept. of Citizenship and Immigration (1956–65); Dept. of Manpower and Immigration (1966–76); and Dept. of Employment and Immigration (1977–84). Figures for 1956–61 based on those of 'Chinese' ethnic origin, and figures for 1962–84 compiled from information on the country of last permanent residence, including China, Hong Kong, and Taiwan.

Most of the post-war Chinese immigrants came in their prime working age, between 15 and 34; Table 6.2 shows that over half of those who came during the periods 1956–67 and 1968–76 belonged to this age group. During the next period (1977–84) 46 per cent were between 15 and 34. Children under 15 accounted for 23 per cent of the Chinese for 1956–67, 18 per cent for 1968–76, and 15 per cent for 1977–84. The higher percentage of children in the first period probably reflected the continuation of family reunification in the 1950s and early 1960s. If one considers children under 15 and adults over 54 as the 'dependent' population, then about 30 per cent of the Chinese immigrants between 1956 and 67 and between 1968 and 1976 belonged to this category. Between 1977 and 1984 the 'dependent' population was about 37 per cent. This is in sharp contrast to the pattern of single Chinese males who came to Canada in the nineteenth and early twentieth centuries. The state has had to pay a higher overhead cost for the post-war immigrants, in terms of providing social and educational services for their dependents, to secure their skilled labour.

Table 6.3 shows the sex ratio of the post-war Chinese immigrants to Canada. The last line indicates that for all three periods there were more female than male Chinese immigrating to Canada. Between 1956 and 1967 there were 65 men to 100 women, largely because of family reunification during this period. The more balanced ratio for 1968–76 reflects the beginning of family migration after the point system for assessing immigrants took effect following 1967. The figures in Table 6.3 also show that for the period 1956–1967 the ratio of men to women decreases as the age group increases. This pattern is consistent with the earlier explanation that many middle-aged and elderly Chinese women joined their husbands after the war. For later periods the sex ratio also declines for higher age groups, but the differences are much less dramatic.

TABLE 6.3

SEX RATIO (MALES PER 100 FEMALES) OF CHINESE
IMMIGRANTS ADMITTED TO CANADA, 1956–84

Age group	1956–67	1968–76	1977–84
0–14	126	111	109
15–34	63	108	88
35–54	46	91	70
55 and over	15	56	81
All age groups	65	98	86

SOURCES: Compiled from annual reports of Dept. of Citizenship and Immigration (1956–65); Dept. of Manpower and Immigration (1966–76); and Dept. of Employment and Immigration (1977–84). Figures for 1956–61 based on those of 'Chinese' ethnic origin, and figures for 1962–84 compiled from information on the country of last permanent residence, including China, Hong Kong, and Taiwan.

TABLE 6.4

INTENDED OCCUPATION OF CHINESE IMMIGRANTS DESTINED
TO THE CANADIAN LABOUR FORCE, 1954–84

Occupations	1954–67 %	1968–76 %	1977–84 %	1954–84 %
Entrepreneurial, managerial, and administrative[a]	3.4	8.4	9.5	8.1
Professional	39.9	28.0	14.9	24.7
Clerical and sales[b]	13.0	23.5	19.5	20.6
Service	27.7	17.3	15.1	17.9
Skilled[c]	8.9	16.3	19.2	16.4
Primary industry and unskilled[d]	6.4	1.6	9.1	5.1
Not classified	0.7	5.0	12.7	7.3
Total	100.0	100.1	100.0	100.1
(Total number of Chinese destined to the Canadian labour force)[e]	(9,664)	(34,649)	(26,676)	(70,989)

SOURCE: Compiled from annual reports of Dept. of Citizenship and Immigration (1954–55); Immigration Statistics, Dept. of Citizenship and Immigration (1956–76); and Immigration Statistics, Dept. of Employment and Immigration (1977–84). Figures for 1954–61 based on those of 'Chinese' ethnic origin, and figures for 1962–84 compiled from information on the country of last permanent residence or country of former residence, including China, Hong Kong, and Taiwan.

a 'Entrepreneurial, managerial, and administrative' occupations include managerial and administrative occupations for 1954–77 and entrepreneurial, managerial, and administrative for 1978–84.

b 'Clerical and sales' occupations include clerical, commercial, and financial occupations for 1954–64; clerical, commercial sales, and financial sales occupations for 1965–72; and clerical and related sales occupations for 1973–84.

c 'Skilled' occupations include manufacturing, mechanical and construction, transportation and communication for 1954–62; manufacturing and mechanical, construction, transport and communication for 1963–72; processing, machining and related, product fabricating, assembling and repairing, construction, transport-equipment operating, material handling and related, and other crafts and equipment operating for 1973–84.

d 'Primary industry' occupations include agricultural, fishing, trapping, logging, and mining for 1954–62; farming, logging, fishing, hunting, trapping, and mining for 1963–72; farming, horticulture and

The post-war immigrants also came with a more diversified occupational background than the earlier immigrants, who were mostly labourers. Table 6.4 shows the intended occupations of the Chinese immigrants between 1954 and 1984. There were a total of 70,989 Chinese destined to the Canadian labour force during this period, of whom about one-quarter were professionals. Clerical and sales occupations made up another 20.6 per cent. In total, the managerial, professional and white-collar occupations accounted for 53 per cent of the Chinese immigrants. About 18 per cent of the post-war Chinese came as service workers, many of whom probably worked in the restaurant and food-service industry. In the post-war period only a small percentage of the Chinese immigrants were unskilled labourers, whereas skilled workers made up 16.4 per cent of the total.

There were some differences in the occupational characteristics of the Chinese immigrants who entered Canada during the three post-war periods. Between 1954 and 1967 those in professional occupations amounted to 40 per cent of the Chinese destined to the labour force. This high percentage reflects the changing demands of the Canadian labour force in the post-war years, especially with respect to trained labour power (Green, 1976). However, the percentage in professional occupations declined to 28 per cent for the period 1968–76, and to 14.9 per cent for 1977–84. This decline was probably related to the fact that Canadian universities were producing more graduates in the 1970s, at a time when the country was experiencing economic recessions. Consequently the need to depend on foreign-trained graduates for the later periods was not as great as during the economic boom years of the 1950s and 1960s.

The changes in the occupational structure of post-war Canada resulted in expansion in both the white-collar and blue-collar sectors, which provided new opportunities for incoming immigrants and enabled the Chinese immigrants to enter occupations

---

animal husbandry, fishing, hunting, trapping and related, mining and quarrying including oil and gas field for 1973–84. The 'Unskilled' category was not reported after 1972.

[e] For 1965 and 1982 there is a discrepancy in the original table between the sum total of Chinese in all occupational groups and the total number of Chinese destined to the labour force. The calculations in this table are based on the sum total of Chinese in all occupational groups.

other than the traditional ones in the service industry. The service occupations, which at one time accounted for the majority of the Chinese in the Canadian labour force, remained the line of employment for 27.7 per cent of the Chinese who immigrated between 1954 and 1967. As more Chinese entered Canada after 1967, however, the percentage in service occupations also declined. The Chinese who came as skilled workers increased from 8.9 per cent for the period 1954–67 to 16.3 per cent for 1968–76, and to 19.2 per cent for 1977–84. Correspondingly, the clerical and sales occupations accounted for 13 per cent of the Chinese immigrants who came between 1954 and 1967, 23.5 per cent between 1968 and 1976, and 19.5 per cent between 1977 and 1984.

In addition to entering a wider range of occupations, the post-war newcomers brought other changes to the Chinese community. As more Chinese immigrated to Canada, conjugal family life was gradually restored, giving rise to a larger second generation (Li, 1980a).[9] In 1981, for the first time in history, the sex ratio among the Chinese community was balanced with 102 men to 100 women. As more Chinese with professional and technical qualifications arrived, the Chinese middle class grew. The geographic boundaries of Chinatowns began to change as more immigrants settled in suburbs. Formerly serving mainly as community centres for the Chinese, Chinatowns now became more commercial areas with high land values. New ethnic associations emerged as the old ones failed to represent the interests of the more heterogeneous Chinese population.

7

Contemporary Chinese-Canadians

By 1981 the Chinese had been in Canada for 123 years, for most of which they were subjected to legislative discrimination and exclusion. It is only in the past three to four decades, since 1947, that the Chinese have been able to enjoy their civil rights as Canadians. With the 1967 changes in immigration policy the Chinese were finally allowed to be admitted under the same conditions as other groups. As more Chinese immigrants came to Canada in the late sixties and the seventies a new Chinese-Canadian community began to emerge. Some of its features can be traced to the history of Chinese immigration to Canada. Others, however, are distinct, reflecting the characteristics of the more recent arrivals.

Social and demographic characteristics

The 1981 Census of Canada reports that out of a total of 24.3 million Canadians, 224,030 claimed Chinese as their mother tongue (Statistics of Canada, 1981a). In terms of ethnic origin, there were 285,800 Chinese in Canada as of 1981 (Table 7.1),[1] about 1 per cent of the total population. The number of Chinese-Canadians in 1981 represents an increase of about 2.5 times that of 1971. This increase is largely attributed to the increase in the volume of Chinese immigration to Canada after 1967 (see Table 6.2). Table 7.1 shows the distribution of Chinese in Canada by provinces. By 1981 British Columbia, with 34.5 per cent, was no longer the province with the largest number of Chinese; 40 per cent resided in Ontario. These two provinces alone accounted for about three-quarters of the Chinese in Canada in 1981. Another 12.8 per cent were located in Alberta and 6.3 per cent in Quebec, with the remaining 6.3 per cent sparsely distributed in Manitoba, Saskatchewan, the Maritimes, Yukon, and the Northwest Territories.

TABLE 7.1

DISTRIBUTION OF CHINESE-CANADIANS BY PROVINCES, 1981

Province	Chinese-Canadians %
Newfoundland	0.3
Nova Scotia	0.5
New Brunswick	0.4
Quebec	6.3
Ontario	40.1
Manitoba	2.6
Saskatchewan	2.3
Alberta	12.8
British Columbia	34.5
Prince Edward Island, Yukon, and Northwest Territories	0.2
Total	100.0
(Number)	(285,800)

SOURCE: Compiled from 1981 Census of Canada, *Public Use Sample Tape, Individual File*. The individual file for 1981 is a 2% probability sample of the total population. Numbers in the table have been weighted to population size.

Like other immigrants to Canada, the Chinese have tended to settle in metropolitan centres. Of the 75 per cent who lived in Ontario and British Columbia, an overwhelming majority resided in Toronto and Vancouver. Together, these two metropolitan centres accounted for 60 per cent of all Chinese in Canada, each having about 85,800 Chinese as of 1981. Cities like Calgary, Edmonton, and Montreal also had sizeable Chinese populations, ranging from 15,000 to 17,000 (Statistics Canada, 1981b).

The majority of the Chinese in Canada remained foreign-born in 1981, as the figures of Table 7.2 indicate. About three-quarters were foreign-born in 1981, as compared with 62 per cent in 1971. The relatively high proportion of foreign-born Chinese is partly a consequence of the unbalanced sex ratio among the Chinese-Canadians in the pre-war years, which delayed the growth of a second generation. But the main reason for the decrease in the

TABLE 7.2

PERIOD OF IMMIGRATION TO CANADA FOR CHINESE-CANADIANS, 1971, 1981

Period	1971 %	1981 %
Before 1946	6.2	1.1
1946–55	11.6	4.4
1956–66	19.9	8.2
1967–71	24.8	13.4
1971–81	—	47.1
Canadian-born	37.6	25.8
Total	100.1	100.0
(Number)	(124,600)	(285,800)

SOURCE: Compiled from 1971 and 1981 Census of Canada, *Public Use Sample Tape, Individual File*. The individual file for 1981 is a 2% probability sample of the total population. Numbers in the table have been weighted to population size.

percentage of Canadian-born Chinese between 1971 and 1981 has to do with the influx of Chinese immigrants to Canada after 1967, which added considerably to the foreign-born segment of the community. Table 7.2 shows that, as of 1971, 24.8 per cent of the Chinese had immigrated to Canada between 1967 and 1971, 20 per cent between 1956 and 1966, and 11.6 per cent between 1946 and 1955. The Chinese who came before 1946 constituted about 6.2 per cent of the Chinese population. By 1981 it becomes clear that most of the Chinese were recent immigrants who had come between 1967 and 1981. Over 60 per cent arrived after 1967, and 47 per cent after 1971. By 1981 only about 13 per cent of the Chinese in Canada had immigrated during the two decades following the war, between 1946 and 1966. The number of Chinese who had come before 1946 had dwindled to 1.1 per cent of the Chinese population.

Table 7.3 shows important differences in the age structure of the foreign-born and native-born components of the Chinese community in 1971 and 1981. For both census years, over 60 per cent of the foreign-born Chinese were between 16 and 45 years old; in contrast, over 60 per cent of the native-born Chinese were under 16. Both the 1971 and 1981 censuses show that about 86 per cent of the native-born Chinese in Canada were under 30. These figures give further support to the claim that the growth of the second and third generation among Chinese-Canadians is a rather recent phenomenon. Table 7.3 also indicates a larger proportion of Chinese in the older age groups among the foreign-born than the native-born Chinese. In 1971, for example, 15.6 per cent of the foreign-born Chinese were between 46 and 65, and 10.7 per cent were 65 and over. In contrast, about 8 per cent of the native-born Chinese were over 45 in 1971. In 1981, 18.5 per cent of the foreign-born Chinese were between 46 and 65, as compared with only 5.3 per cent of the native-born Chinese in this age category. Likewise, 7.3 per cent of the foreign-born Chinese, as compared with 1.7 per cent of the native-born ones, were 65 and over in 1981.

The large percentage of recent Chinese immigrants has had many social implications. Historically, despite the mistreatment they suffered, there was a conspicuous absence of Chinese influ-

TABLE 7.3

AGE COMPOSITION OF FOREIGN-BORN AND NATIVE-BORN
CHINESE-CANADIANS, 1971, 1981

	Foreign-born		Native-born	
Age	1971 %	1981 %	1971 %	1981 %
Under 16	13.2	12.9	65.4	61.9
16–29	27.5	29.1	20.1	24.9
30–45	33.0	32.1	6.2	6.2
46–65	15.6	18.5	6.8	5.3
65 and over	10.7	7.3	1.5	1.7
Total	100.0	99.9	100.0	100.0
(Number)	(77,800)	(212,650)	(46,800)	(73,150)

SOURCE: Compiled from 1971 and 1981 Census of Canada, *Public Use Sample Tape, Individual File*. The individual file for 1981 is a 2% probability sample of the total population. Numbers in the table have been weighted to population size.

ence in Canadian politics. It is only in recent years that they have begun to organize protest movements to press for social equality.[2] Undoubtedly the large number of recent immigrants, the small number of Canadian-born Chinese, and their relatively young age together explain why the Chinese are hesitant in entering Canadian politics and cautious in demanding greater equality.

The recent Chinese immigrants also bring other changes to the Chinese community. With more Chinese in professional and technical occupations entering Canada (see Table 6.4), many are choosing the suburbs, not the Chinatowns, as the place to live. At the same time, the growth of the Chinese population in many cities provides a larger ethnic clientèle for the Chinese businesses in Chinatowns. Hence there has been both an expansion of the Chinatown areas in cities like Toronto and Vancouver and a proliferation of Chinese in residential neighbourhoods. A study of immigrants based largely on census materials indicates that of twenty-one ethnic groups in Montreal, Toronto, Winnipeg, and Vancouver the Chinese were among the five with the highest degree of residential segregation (Richmond and Kalbach, 1980: 189). In the case of Vancouver the index of segregation[3] for Chinese was 54.0, the second highest among the twenty-one ethnic groups. In Toronto the index of segregation for Chinese was 49.3, ranking fourth highest. These findings suggest that although the majority of the Chinese do not reside in Chinatowns per se (Reitz, 1980: 91), they tend to live in areas with a relatively high concentration of members of the same ethnic group. Using mother tongue to classify the Chinese, the data from the 1981 Census indicate that the ten census tracts in Vancouver with the highest concentration of Chinese accounted for 28 per cent of the total Chinese in the city, and that Chinatown was not among these tracts (Statistics Canada, 1981a). These patterns indicate that despite the public image of Chinatowns as centres of Chinese communities, in fact only a small percentage of the Chinese now reside in such areas.

There are many indications that the Chinatowns in major cities today have lost many of the functions they once performed for Chinese residents. A recent study of Chinatown and Chinese businesses in Vancouver confirms the fact that although China-town enjoys a public image of an ethnic enclave, only 20 per cent of the Chinese-owned firms are in fact located in the neighbour-hood, and few Chinese live there (Li, 1983a). Certain types of

Chinese-owned businesses, such as food-service, merchandising, and retail operations, are more likely to be found in Chinatown than are grocery stores, which are more often located outside. The case of Vancouver Chinatown suggests that the major value of Chinatown to Chinese businesses is its commercial appeal as a tourist attraction, which, from the point of view of marketing, is a good strategy to promote ethnic goods and services. From the point of view of consumers, it offers an ethnic component that gives an added flavour and novelty to what would otherwise be another plain commercial block. In this sense the Chinatown today is more of a commercial district marketing ethnic goods and services, and less of a cultural community. Consequently, despite its higher land value, the Chinatown as a commercial area appeals to those Chinese entrepreneurs who market ethnic food and products and thus benefit from the tourist image of Chinatown as an ethnic enclave (Li, 1983a).

Aside from the changes in the residential patterns, other characteristics of the Chinese community reflect that its population is composed of many recent immigrants. In terms of maintaining social ties within the ethnic group, a study based on a probability sample reports that 79.7 per cent of the Chinese respondents indicated that they maintained close friendship ties and a high level of social visiting with members of the same ethnic group (Reitz, 1980: 109–21). The same study indicates that 82.2 per cent of the Chinese identified with their ethnic origin (Reitz, 1980: 121). These findings are consistent with what would be expected from an ethnic community with a large foreign-born population.

Other statistics show that there were thirty-six headquarters of Chinese cultural organizations in Canada in 1974 (Statistics Canada, 1974: 282), and that the Chinese ranked fifth highest in the number of such organizations, after the Italians, Poles, Germans, and Ukrainians.[4] Clanship and locality associations have declined in importance, as they can no longer use the same surname or locality to appeal to the new Chinese immigrants who have come from diverse social and geographical origins. Likewise, the secret societies are unable to respond to the needs of the recent immigrants the way they did to those of Chinese workers in the nineteenth century. Consequently membership in these associations has declined drastically in recent years, and the nature of their operations has changed to performing mainly social functions for their aging members.

Linguistic characteristics

In a comparison with other ethnic groups in Canada, the Chinese have shown the highest rate of language retention (see de Vries and Vallee, 1980: 103); this observation is consistent with a high percentage of Chinese-Canadians being foreign-born. The 1981 Census shows that over 75 per cent indicated the Chinese language as their mother tongue, while 21.6 per cent claimed English (Table 7.4). The table also shows that 63 per cent reported Chinese as the language most often spoken at home in 1981, while 35 per cent cited English.

TABLE 7.4

MOTHER TONGUE AND LANGUAGE MOST OFTEN SPOKEN AT HOME, FOR CHINESE-CANADIANS, 1981

Language	Mother tongue %	Language most often spoken at home %
English	21.6	34.5
French	0.5	0.5
Chinese	75.2	62.6
Other	2.8	2.3
Total	100.1	99.9
(Number)	(285,800)	(285,800)

SOURCE: Compiled from 1981 Census of Canada, *Public Use Sample Tape, Individual File*. The individual file for 1981 is a 2% probability sample of the total population. Numbers in the table have been weighted to population size.

Despite a high level of language retention among the Chinese, there is a certain degree of language loss.[5] Table 7.4 shows that the percentage of Chinese using English as the home language (34.5 per cent) is larger than that claiming English as mother tongue (21.6 per cent). Specifically , among those whose mother tongue was Chinese there were 78 per cent who still used Chinese as the home language in 1981. In short, 22 per cent of the Chinese had experienced a language shift in the current generation. When comparisons are made between the native-born and foreign-born Chinese, the data of the 1981 Census show that the problem of language loss is more severe among the native-born. For example, 82 per cent of the foreign-born were able to maintain Chinese as the language most often spoken at home, as compared with 56 per cent among the native-born (Statistics Canada, 1981b). These figures reflect the forces of linguistic assimilation and the increasing difficulty, for linguistic minorities, of maintaining their language in subsequent generations.

Data on mother tongue and home language alone, however, are not sufficient to ascertain the potential linguistic difficulty that some Chinese-Canadians encounter in bilingual Canada. Table 7.5 provides information on the extent to which Chinese-Canadians are officially bilingual, that is, are capable of speaking either or both of the official languages. In 1981 the officially bilingual population among the Chinese was quite small, amounting to only 4.3 per cent of all Chinese-Canadians. In contrast, 75.9 per cent of Chinese-Canadians were officially unilingual English, and only 0.6 per cent unilingual French. Those speaking neither English nor French accounted for 19.2 per cent of all Chinese-Canadians. This means that approximately one out of

TABLE 7.5

OFFICIAL BILINGUALISM AMONG FOREIGN-BORN AND
NATIVE-BORN CHINESE-CANADIANS, 1981

| | Chinese-Canadians | | |
Official language	Foreign-born %	Native-born %	Total %
English only	73.8	81.9	75.9
French only	0.8	0.1	0.6
Both English and French	3.7	5.9	4.3
Neither English nor French	21.6	12.0	19.2
Total	99.9	99.9	100.0
(Number)	(212,650)	(73,150)	(285,800)

SOURCE: Compiled from 1981 Census of Canada, *Public Use Sample Tape, Individual File*. The individual file for 1981 is a 2% probability sample of the total population. Numbers in the table have been weighted to population size.

every five Chinese-Canadians would likely encounter language barriers in Canadian society. The percentage of Chinese who spoke neither English nor French was higher among those born outside of Canada than those born inside. But even among the native-born Chinese-Canadians 12 per cent spoke neither one of the two official languages. The Chinese-Canadians who spoke neither English nor French must have become highly dependent on the ethnic enclave for providing basic services.

The contemporary Chinese-Canadian family

With the increase in Chinese women coming to Canada after the war and more Chinese immigrating as a family unit, especially after 1967, conjugal family life was restored in the Chinese-Canadian community. By 1971 an overwhelming majority of Chinese in Canada belonged to a nuclear family. The 1971 Census shows that 83 per cent of the Chinese in Canada belonged to a census family household, which is composed of a husband and wife with or without unmarried children, or a single parent with unmarried children. In contrast, 6.5 per cent of the Chinese belonged to an economic family, which includes parents living with their married child and his or her family. Individual Chinese not belonging to a family made up only about 10 per cent of the total (Li, 1983b). If the percentages of individuals in different types of family are used as a rough indication of the family organization, the 1971 Census data indicate that the nuclear family is the dominant pattern among the Chinese-Canadians. Furthermore, in comparison with all Canadians, the percentage of Chinese-Canadians belonging to a census family (83.1 per cent) is only slightly less than the national figure of 87.4 per cent.

Concerning the average family size, the 1971 Census shows that the average number of persons in the census family was 4.63 for Chinese-Canadians and 4.50 for all Canadians. The average number of children born to adult married women was 2.63 for Chinese-Canadians, as compared with 2.77 for all Canadian women (Li, 1983b). These statistics suggest that the Chinese-Canadian family in 1971 was quite similar to the average Canadian family with respect to family size and fertility of married women.

Table 7.6 provides further evidence on the types of household for Chinese-Canadians and other Canadians, based on the 1981

Census. The data show that 50.6 per cent of Chinese-Canadians, as compared with 70.7 per cent of other Canadians, belonged to the husband-wife family household. In contrast, there was a higher percentage of Chinese-Canadians in the husband-wife family household with additional persons (19.6 per cent) than other Canadians (7.3 per cent). These differences suggest that although over 70 per cent of the Chinese-Canadians and other Canadians belonged to the husband-wife family, the Chinese were more likely to have additional persons, other than children, living with them. When the nativity of Chinese-Canadians is taken into account, the 1981 data show that 48 per cent of the

TABLE 7.6

TYPES OF HOUSEHOLD FOR CHINESE-CANADIANS AND
OTHER CANADIANS, 1981

Individuals belonging to:	Chinese-Canadians %	Other Canadians %
Husband-wife family household with or without children	50.6	70.7
Husband-wife family household (with or without children), with additional persons	19.6	7.3
Lone-parent family households	5.7	7.9
Secondary family households	3.1	1.4
Multiple family households	12.5	2.1
Non-family households	8.3	10.7
Total	99.8	100.1
(Total individuals)	(282,750)	(23,519,750)

SOURCE: Compiled from 1981 Census of Canada, *Public Use Sample Tape, Individual File*. The Individual File for 1981 is a 2% probability sample of the total population. Numbers in the table have been weighted to population size.

foreign-born Chinese, as compared with 58 per cent of the native-born Chinese, belonged to the husband-wife family household without additional persons (Statistics Canada, 1981b). These patterns suggest a greater tendency for a nuclear family among native-born than foreign-born Chinese. Table 7.6 also shows that 12.5 per cent of the Chinese-Canadians, as compared with only 2.1 per cent of other Canadians, belonged to the multiple family household, that is, a household with one or more families occupying the same dwelling. Furthermore, 3.1 per cent of the Chinese-Canadians, in contrast to 1.4 per cent of other Canadians, were members of the secondary family household.[6] The 1981 Census data display some interesting differences between the types of households for Chinese-Canadians and other Canadians. It is not clear whether these differences are characteristic of recent immigrants or of ethnic culture. But there are indications that the differences are likely to be reduced in subsequent generations of Chinese-Canadians.

On the basis of the foregoing data it is possible to make some general remarks about the contemporary Chinese-Canadian family. Although Chinese-Canadians are similar to other Canadians regarding family size and fertility rate, there are some differences in household type. Chinese-Canadians are more likely than other Canadians to have multiple families living in the same dwelling, or to be living in the husband-wife family household with additional persons other than their children. But, in contrast to the broken families common among many Chinese immigrants before the war, an overwhelming majority of post-war Chinese-Canadians are now living in conjugal families.

Changing characteristics of the Chinese-Canadian community

Although the Chinese had been coming to Canada since 1858, by the 1930s and 1940s the Chinese community was shrinking and aging as a result of a long period of legislative controls and exclusionary measures on the part of the Canadian government. Surviving through the era of exclusion, the community slowly began to grow as the Chinese gained more civil rights after the war and immigration laws permitted more to come to Canada. These changes were produced in part by the economic conditions of Canada after the Second World War, which were characterized by rapid industrial expansion and the resulting demand for skilled labour. When the law allowed them to apply as independent immigrants, a larger volume of Chinese, coming from a more heterogeneous background, immigrated to Canada. The subsequent growth of a new Chinese community was made possible through a new wave of immigration after the 1967 change in immigration policy. Today the Chinese-Canadian community is made up largely of recent immigrants who came to Canada in the past two decades. Although with the increase in family migration a generation of Canadian-born Chinese has emerged, it remains relatively young.

With the arrival of recent immigrants the married-bachelor society among Chinese-Canadians has been gradually replaced by conjugal families. The majority of Chinese-Canadians, however, remain foreign-born, because of the long delay of the second generation and the rise in numbers of post-war immigrants. The high percentage of foreign-born means that the Chinese-Canadians share many characteristics of other recent immigrants, despite their presence in Canada since the middle of the nineteenth century. Among these characteristics are the high percentage of those retaining the ethnic language as mother tongue and home language, and the high proportion of the second and third generations under the age of sixteen. The inability of many Chinese-Canadians to speak either one of the official languages implies that severe language problems remain for a segment of the community in adjusting to Canadian society.

The Chinatown has ceased to be the centre of the Chinese community as there has been less pressure of segregation in recent decades, compared with the pre-war years. Undoubtedly the improved public attitude towards the Chinese, together with their educational and occupational accomplishments, has enabled many to move into middle-class white neighbourhoods. Many clan and district associations, which played an important role in the lives of early Chinese immigrants, have declined in importance as they no longer meet the needs of the new immigrants. In their place new Chinese associations that appeal to a broader community base are emerging. Finally, despite the growth of the Chinese community, the Chinese have been cautious in entering Canadian politics and demanding greater equality in Canadian society.

8

Social Mobility and Inequality

With the emergence of a new community after the war and the diversification of the lines of work open to its members, it is tempting to accept the success of the Chinese as the final fulfilment of the mobility dream. Propagated in the middle of the nineteenth century, the mobility dream was the quest of many European immigrants who crossed the Atlantic in search of a better life in the New World. The chief tenet of the mobility dream was equal opportunities for all: immigrants became the architects of their own fortune (Thernstrom, 1972: 57–64; Lipset and Bendix, 1966: 76–91). Individual entrepreneurship and perseverance were the keys to success in the New World, where social status was supposedly determined by achievement, not ascription. Historically, the mobility dream remained a romantic ideal for many immigrants, as long as Canada was stratified into unequal statuses of charter and immigrant groups (Porter, 1965). With the repeal of discriminatory laws and the gradual acceptance of Chinese into Canadian society, there was hope that the mobility dream might be finally realized by the Chinese in Canada. It was in reaction to the success of the post-war immigrants that a journalist wrote in *Maclean's* in 1977:

> Ah, the Chinese. Ever resourceful, ever industrious and doing ever so well. Especially here in *Guam Sann* (Golden Mountain) now that the top of the mountain is in view. (Miller, 1977: 42p)

Certainly the Chinese have made many strides in post-war Canada, especially in the area of civil rights and job opportunity. But it would be incorrect to assume, on the grounds of educational and occupational mobility, that race is no longer a barrier for Chinese-Canadians.

Social mobility

There is little doubt that comparisons between the occupational patterns of Chinese-Canadians today and fifty years ago show substantial upward mobility. For example, 57 per cent of the employed Chinese workers in 1921, and 61 per cent in 1931, were servants, janitors, laundry and restaurant workers, and unskilled

TABLE 8.1

OCCUPATIONS OF CHINESE IN THE EMPLOYED LABOUR FORCE OF CANADA, 15 YEARS OF AGE AND OVER, 1971, 1981

Occupations	1971 %	1981 %
Managerial, administrative, and related occupations	1.2	4.9
Professional and technical occupations	17.8	17.8
Clerical and related occupations	11.0	18.5
Sales occupations	10.8	7.5
Transport-equipment operating occupations	0.8	1.4
Processing, machining, and construction occupations	11.8	16.5
Service occupations	27.9	24.5
Farming and other primary occupations	2.2	1.0
Other occupations	4.8	3.7
Occupations not stated	11.8	4.2
Total	100.1%	100%
(Number)	(50,100)	(168,100)

SOURCE: Compiled from 1971, 1981 Census of Canada, *Public Use Sample Tape, Individual File,* excluding persons under 15 years, persons who have not worked since the previous year, and inmates. The individual file for 1981 is a 2% probability sample of the total population. The individual file for 1971 Census is a 1% probability sample of the total population, excluding Prince Edward Island, Yukon, and the Northwest Territories. Numbers in the table have been weighted to population size.

workers (see Table 3.2). Lately, although service occupations still employed the largest number of Chinese workers, their relative importance has declined to 28 per cent of employed Chinese in 1971, and to 24.5 per cent in 1981 (Table 8.1). In contrast, less than 1 per cent of the Chinese work force in 1921 and 1931 was in professional occupations. In the census years of 1971 and 1981 the professional and technical occupations constituted 18 per cent of all employed Chinese. There were also substantial gains in the white-collar occupations. While clerical and related occupations were almost non-existent among the Chinese in 1921 and 1931, they accounted for 11 per cent of those employed in 1971, and 18.5 per cent in 1981. Likewise, whereas at the turn of the twentieth century they were excluded from the skilled occupations in many sectors, they have made substantial headway in the blue-collar sector in recent decades. In 1971 about 12 per cent of the employed Chinese held jobs in processing, machining, and construction; by 1981 these jobs accounted for 16 per cent of the employed Chinese. These statistics give the impression that the Chinese have overcome the obstacles of historical racism and have successfully advanced into the core labour market. As we will see, however, that impression is not supported by other evidence.

Even compared with other Canadians, the Chinese-Canadians have done well educationally and occupationally. For example, Table 8.2 shows that in 1981 there was a higher percentage of Chinese-Canadians than other Canadians with a university education; about 29 per cent had at least some university, as compared with about 16 per cent among the rest of the population. The Chinese (17.5 per cent) were more than twice as likely as other Canadians (7.9 per cent) to have completed university, and the rate was slightly higher for those born outside of Canada (17.7 per cent) than for the native-born (16 per cent). These figures point to a large percentage of Chinese at the highest educational level and suggest that the foreign-born contributed substantially to this achievement. Comparing those with some high school or less, Table 8.2 also shows fewer Chinese (43.9 per cent) than other Canadians (47.8 per cent) at this educational level. Here, however, the percentage was higher among those Chinese born outside (45.5 per cent) than in Canada (34 per cent).

TABLE 8.2

LEVEL OF SCHOOLING FOR FOREIGN-BORN AND NATIVE-
BORN CHINESE-CANADIANS AND OTHER CANADIANS,
15 YEARS OF AGE AND OVER, 1981

| Level of schooling | Chinese-Canadians | | | Other Canadians |
	Foreign-born %	Native-born %	Total %	%
Some high school or less	45.5	34.0	43.9	47.8
Completed high school	10.8	13.2	11.1	16.6
Trade school	16.0	17.1	16.1	19.8
Some university	10.0	19.7	11.3	17.9
Completed university	17.7	16.0	17.5	7.9
Total	100.0	100.0	99.9	100.0
(Number)	(187,800)	(29,450)	(217,250)	(18,389,250)

SOURCE: Compiled from 1981 Census of Canada, *Public Use Sample Tape, Individual File.* The individual file for 1981 is a 2% probability sample of the total population. Numbers in the table have been weighted to population size.

Concerning occupational achievement, the 1981 Census shows that the Chinese were no longer under-represented in manage-rial, professional, and other white-collar occupations, although they were still over-represented in service jobs (Table 8.3). While the Chinese had a slightly lower percentage (4.8 per cent) than other Canadians (6.4 per cent) in managerial and administrative positions, 17.8 per cent were in professional and technical jobs, as compared with 14.5 per cent of other Canadians. In terms of other white-collar occupations, the Chinese were just as likely as other Canadians to be in clerical jobs, and only slightly under-represented in sales occupations. But they were clearly under-represented in such blue-collar occupations as processing, machining, construction, and transport-equipment operating.

TABLE 8.3

OCCUPATIONS OF FOREIGN-BORN AND NATIVE-BORN
CHINESE-CANADIANS AND OTHER CANADIANS, 1981

| Occupations | Chinese-Canadians | | | Other |
	Foreign-born %	Native-born %	Total %	%
Managerial, administrative, and related occupations	4.6	6.6	4.8	6.4
Professional and technical occupations	18.1	15.9	17.8	14.5
Clerical and related occupations	17.0	28.0	18.5	18.5
Sales occupations	6.5	13.8	7.5	9.7
Transport-equipment operating occupations	1.0	3.6	1.4	3.6
Processing, machining, and construction occupations	17.8	7.9	16.4	20.1
Service occupations	26.3	14.0	24.5	12.3
Farming and other primary occupations	0.9	1.9	1.0	6.1
Other occupations	3.6	4.0	3.7	5.0
Occupations not stated	4.2	4.2	4.2	3.8
Total	100.0	99.9	99.8	100.0
(Number)	(144,550)	(23,550)	(168,100)	(12,995,550)

SOURCE: Compiled from 1981 Census of Canada, *Public Use Sample Tape, Individual File.* The individual file for 1981 is a 2% probability sample of the total population. Numbers in the table have been weighted to population size.

About 18 per cent of the employed Chinese were in these lines of work in 1981, as compared with 24 per cent among other Canadians. The Chinese were twice as probable as other Canadians in service jobs, which accounted for about a quarter of the

Chinese in the labour force in 1981. These statistics are in sharp contrast to the exclusion period, when the Chinese were employed almost entirely in unskilled and service jobs.

Despite their diversification into more prestigious jobs, the service industry, particularly food service, has remained an important sector of employment for many Chinese. The 1981 Census data show that 24 per cent of the employed Chinese were in service occupations, as compared with 13 per cent of other Canadians (Statistics Canada, 1981b). The Chinese were particularly over-represented in accommodation and food services, with 21 per cent of those employed working in this sector as compared with 6 per cent of other Canadians (Statistics Canada, 1981b). These figures probably suggest that later cohorts of Chinese immigrants have had a tendency to enter those occupations that previous groups have shown to be successful, and that the service occupations remain a safe haven for those Chinese without professional and technical qualifications.

There are other differences in the ways the foreign-born and native-born Chinese were distributed in the occupational categories. For example, the foreign-born were more likely to be in professional and technical jobs, but less likely to be in managerial and administrative jobs, than the native-born Chinese. In other white-collar fields 28 per cent of the native-born Chinese were in clerical and related occupations, whereas only 17 per cent of the foreign-born were in these jobs. But there is clearly a higher percentage of foreign- than native-born Chinese in blue-collar and service occupations. For example, 26.3 per cent of the foreign-born, as compared with 14 per cent of the native-born, were in service occupations. Whereas 18.8 per cent of the foreign-born were in jobs related to processing, machining, construction and transport-equipment operating, only 11.5 per cent of the native-born Chinese were in these occupations. These differences reflect in part the process of social mobility for the native-born Chinese and in part the selective recruitment of first-generation immigrants. While it is quite true that a substantial percentage of the native-born Chinese were able to stay away from service and blue-collar occupations and move into clerical and professional jobs, their representation in professional occupations was less than that of the foreign-born. The emphasis on educational qualification as a criterion for immigration in the post-war period means that many recent Chinese immigrants to Canada have been admitted because of their educational and professional expertise (see Table 6.4). This fact accounts for the high concentration of foreign-born Chinese in professional and technical jobs. At the same time, the high concentration of foreign-born Chinese in service jobs reflects the continuing importance of the restaurant and service industry to first-generation immigrants.

Data on home ownership from the 1981 Census also show that the Chinese were doing extremely well in comparison with other Canadians. For example, 73 per cent, as compared with 70.5 per cent of other Canadians, lived in a dwelling that was owned by some member of the household (Statistics Canada, 1981b). But the Chinese were more likely than other Canadians to own expensive dwellings: in 1981 about 26 per cent lived in owner-occupied dwellings worth between $100,000 and $149,000, as compared with 12 per cent among other Canadians. Furthermore, 34 per cent of the Chinese, as compared with 10 per cent of other Canadians, were in a household that owned a dwelling worth over $150,000 (Statistics Canada, 1981b). These accomplishments show that the Chinese-Canadians have indeed come a long way, from an inferior position during the exclusion era to a respectable social status in contemporary Canadian society.

Structural forces of social mobility

While the Chinese-Canadians have made spectacular socio-economic advances in recent decades, much of their mobility has to do with overall changes in the occupational structure of Canada after the war, as it changed from an agricultural economy to a capitalist power. In other words, the improved opportunities of the Chinese after the war have more to do with the industrial expansion of Canada than with the social equality implied in the mobility dream. There is much evidence that Canada has experienced major occupational shifts in the last hundred years. For example, close to half of the working-age population[1] in 1881 was engaged in agricultural pursuits. But the segment of the labour force in agriculture dropped to 40 per cent in 1901, 29 per cent in 1931, 16 per cent in 1951, and under 6 per cent in 1971 (Statistics Canada, 1983: D1–7). At the same time, the proportion of the labour force that was employed by the government increased from less than 3 per cent in 1911 to over 8 per cent in 1971. Those employed in educational, health, and welfare services jumped from 3 per cent of the labour force in 1911 to about 13 per cent in 1971 (Statistics Canada, 1983: D56–85). These changes reflect the demise of agriculture as a major sector of employment and the corresponding industrial expansion that produced more opportunities in white-collar and service jobs. The data on the relative increases of output in various industries also reflect the impact of industrialization. For example, between 1935 and 1976 the real domestic product[2] in constant values[3] increased 7.6 times. However, the real domestic product in agriculture only doubled between 1935 and 1976, whereas the increase for the same period in manufacturing industries was 9.8 times, in construction 11 times, and in trade 9 times (Statistics Canada, 1983: F225–40).

Given Canada's industrial growth, especially following the Second World War, it is evident that post-war immigrants in general have better opportunities than those who came earlier in the century. But these improved opportunities may have little to do with greater equality. If many recent Chinese immigrants landed immediately in professional and skilled occupations, it is only because they entered Canada at a time when their technical expertise answered the structural demands of the labour market. The evidence from the U.S., Canada, Austria, England, and Wales clearly suggests that when changes in the occupational structure are taken into consideration, the pattern of inter-generational mobility has remained virtually unchanged (Hauser and Featherman, 1977; McRoberts and Selbee, 1981).

In many ways the changes in immigration policy in 1962 and 1967 (see Chapter 6) were in response to the labour needs created in Canada as a result of industrial expansion. The changes in immigration policy in 1967 stressed in particular the importance of educational and occupational qualifications as criteria for accepting immigrants to Canada. Earlier, Canada had been losing many professional and technical workers to the United States, as the post-war industrial boom there also demanded a large volume of skilled labour; between 1953 and 1963 there was a net outflow of 41,263 professional workers and 38,363 skilled workers from Canada to the U.S. (Parai, 1965: 47–57). However, Canada was able to maintain a net gain of 125,242 professional and skilled workers for the same period only because of a larger volume of those workers immigrating to Canada from around the world. Between 1950 and 1963 Canada was experiencing an average annual outflow of 5,476 professional workers to the U.S. and the United Kingdom. Despite an average volume of 7,790 professional workers every year immigrating to Canada from around the world, the average net gain per year was only 2,314 professional workers (Parai, 1965: 33). These structural conditions compelled Canada to change its policy in 1967 to facilitate the immigration of professional and technical workers. As a result many Chinese immigrants with educational and professional credentials entered Canada. These structural forces provided the conditions for a middle class of professionals and white-collar workers to develop in the Chinese community in Canada. The growth of this middle class was also facilitated by the upward mobility of the native-born Chinese-Canadians, as a segment of them matured and managed to move into professional and technical jobs.

The cost of being Chinese in the Canadian labour market

It is premature to claim, on the basis of social mobility brought about by structural changes, that the Chinese have finally realized the mobility dream. Using the 1981 Census data, it is possible to assess whether they have encountered racial discrimination in the labour market. If the Chinese are enjoying the same opportunities as other ethnic groups in Canada, then their racial origin should have no bearing on their earnings, especially when inter-group differences in schooling, social class, and other factors have been taken into account. The 1981 Census indicates that, despite the educational and occupational mobility of the Chinese, they have not attained income equality relative to other ethnic origins. While the average schooling for all Canadians was 11.56 years, for Chinese-Canadians it was 12.12 (Statistics Canada, 1981b). However, when the economic return of schooling is calculated in terms of annual earnings, those of Jewish or British origin received a higher return on each additional year of schooling than those of Chinese or black origin.[4] Consequently income inequality widens as the educational level increases, because the income differential at each educational level is cumulated to the next level. In other words, even though Chinese-Canadians had attained the same educational level as other groups, their income was less than what the same educational level would have earned Canadians of Jewish or British origin.

Table 8.4 presents a more systematic picture of the cost of being Chinese-Canadian in the Canadian labour market. The effect of ethnic origin on annual earnings is measured in deviations above (plus sign) or below (minus sign) the national average (mean) income. These deviations make it possible to assess the magnitude of income inequality associated with each ethnic origin. A deviation above the mean indicates that there is a bonus or reward for that ethnic group in the labour market, whereas a deviation below shows that the given ethnic group suffers a penalty.[5] Column 2 of the table shows the gross effects of ethnic origin on earnings, that is, the actual differences in income that are associated with each ethnic origin when variations in other factors are not controlled for. The figures indicate that, with the exception of French-Canadians, all European groups had annual earnings above the national average of $14,045. This suggests that Canadians of European origin have an advantage over other groups in the labour market. On average the Chinese had an income level $1,295 below the national average. Part of this income disparity, no doubt, resulted from variations in other factors, such as differences in schooling. Column 3 shows the net effect of ethnic origin on income, when inter-group differences in nativity, age, gender, schooling, social class, sectors, and the number of weeks worked have been adjusted for.[6] The data show clearly that, despite controlling for these variations, the Chinese earned $821 less than an average Canadian in the labour force. The fact that the Chinese who worked in the same sector for the same number of weeks as other Canadians of the same schooling, age, gender, social class, and nativity status did not receive as much income as other Canadians shows that there is a price to being Chinese in the Canadian labour market. In 1981 the average Chinese in Canada suffered an income loss of $821 that can be directly attributed to the person's racial origin. This price, or the cost of discrimination, is one of the highest among seventeen ethnic groups, second only to what the blacks had to pay in the labour market. These findings suggest that race remains a salient factor in determining income inequality. If the Chinese have overcome the historical obstacles of racism, they have yet to cross the barriers of racial discrimination in the Canadian labour market.

Historically, when confronted with racial hostility and market discrimination the Chinese avoided competition with white

TABLE 8.4

GROSS AND NET EFFECTS[a] OF ETHNIC ORIGIN ON ANNUAL
EARNINGS

Ethnic origin	(1) Number	(2) Gross effect ($)	(3) Net effect[b] ($)
Jewish	3,185	6,261.64	3,230.61
Portuguese	2,084	−2,001.94	1,420.89
Scandinavian	3,533	1859.80	787.38
Italian	8,862	−509.41	542.27
Croatian[c]	1,432	458.64	491.32
German	14,175	652.37	184.77
Ukrainian	6,507	794.66	55.83
Dutch	5,036	311.28	24.31
Czech and Slovak	850	2,136.94	6.88
British	107,305	355.81	−20.40
French	66,676	−501.11	−112.87
Hungarian	1,435	1,901.63	−122.23
Other[d]	32,208	−1113.34	−226.21
Polish	3,230	720.78	−251.68
Greek	1,675	−1,893.87	−661.34
Chinese	3,362	−1,294.63	−821.28
Black[e]	1,718	−1,587.96	−1,626.81
All groups	263,273	14,044.87	14,044.87

SOURCE: Compiled from 1981 Census of Canada, *Public Use Sample Tape,
Individual File,* excluding persons under 15 years, persons who have
not worked since January 1, 1980, and inmates. The individual file is
a 2% sample of the total population. Numbers in the table are the same
as those provided in the 2% sample.
[a] Gross and net effects are measured as deviations from the grand mean
income, using Multiple Classification Analysis (Andrews et al., 1976).
[b] Inter-group differences in nativity, gender, age, schooling, social
class, sectors, and the number of weeks worked have been adjusted.
[c] Includes Croatian, Serbian, Slovene, and Yugoslav.
[d] Includes other single origins and all multiple origins.
[e] Includes African, Caribbean, Canadian black, and other black.

Canadians by retreating into an ethnic economic enclave (see
Chapter 3). The Chinese laundries, and later restaurants, sym-
bolized the success of the Chinese in adapting to a racially antag-
onistic market. Despite the removal of statutory discrimination

in the post-war years and the subsequent educational and occupational mobility of more recent immigrants, the Chinese continue to face economic discrimination in the Canadian labour market. The occupational pattern from the 1981 Census suggests that the Chinese have adapted to the Canadian economy by concentrating on certain lines of work that tend to minimize their racial handicap. Even in the professional occupations, they have a tendency to enter scientific and engineering fields, which demand technical expertise, as opposed to other fields requiring more social interaction and different social skills. Table 8.5 compares the Chinese-Canadians with other Canadians in profes-

TABLE 8.5

DISTRIBUTION OF CHINESE-CANADIANS AND OTHER
CANADIANS IN PROFESSIONAL OCCUPATIONS, 1981

Professional occupation	Chinese-Canadians %	Other Canadians %
Occupations in natural sciences, engineering, and mathematics	48.5	21.1
Occupations in social sciences and related fields	4.7	10.7
Teaching and related occupations	12.6	28.3
Occupations in medicine and health	27.7	29.6
Artistic, literary, recreational, and related occupations	6.5	10.2
Total	100.0	99.9
(Number)	(30,850)	(1,944,950)

SOURCE: Compiled from 1981 Census of Canada, *Public Use Sample Tape, Individual File,* excluding persons under 15 years, persons who have not worked since January 1, 1980, and inmates. The individual file is a 2% probability sample of the total population. Numbers in the table have been weighted to population size.

sional occupations. The data show that in 1981, 49 per cent of the Chinese-Canadians in professional occupations were in jobs related to science, engineering and mathematics, as compared with 21 per cent of other Canadians. In contrast, Chinese-Canadians were under-represented in teaching and the social sciences. Although the census data are inconclusive, they indicate an occupational pattern supporting the notion that the Chinese have entered certain lines of work to avoid disadvantageous competition because of their racial background.

Athough there is no longer any statutory discrimination against the Chinese in Canada, they are not immune from racial prejudice in Canadian society. In a national survey conducted in 1974, for example, Canadians were asked to rate nineteen ethnic groups on whether each group was considered by the respondents as hardworking, important, Canadian, clean, likeable, and interesting. The Chinese received the unfavourable rating of fifteenth among the nineteen ethnic groups (Berry, Kalin and Taylor, 1977). Another survey, conducted in 1978 in a western Canadian city, shows that close to 10 per cent of the respondents considered that Canada had been harmed by Chinese coming into the country and that 27 per cent were opposed to Chinese immigrating to Canada (Li, 1979b). In 1974 an editorial in the *Medical Post* gave a stereotyped description of Chinese medical students and supported a prejudiced stance to curb the number of Chinese students in the medical school at the University of Toronto (cited in Mah, 1976). At that time there were 33 Chinese, most of them were landed immigrants, out of 241 students admitted to first-year medical studies (Mah, 1976).

Periodic instances remind the Chinese that, despite their accomplishments in Canada, they are often seen as foreigners by the Canadian public. On September 30, 1979, on its public-affairs program *W5*, the CTV television network broadcast a report on foreign students in Canada under the title 'Campus Giveaway'. The program incorrectly reported that at least 100,000 foreign students were taking away university openings that could have gone to qualified Canadian students,[7] and showed many scenes with crowds of Chinese students in Canadian university classrooms. By implication the Chinese students, irrespective of nationality, were equated with foreign students allegedly taking educational opportunities away from white Canadians. Massive demonstrations (*Globe and Mail*, Jan. 28, 1980) and vigorous lobbying by Chinese-Canadians finally forced the network to issue an apology to the Chinese on April 16, 1980. In it Mr. Murray Chercover, President and Managing Director of the CTV Television Network, said that

> our critics—particularly Chinese Canadians and the universities—criticized the program as racist: they were right. . . . There is no doubt that the distorted statistics, combined with our visual presentation, made the program appear racist in tone and effect. . . . We sincerely apologize for the fact that Chinese Canadians were depicted as foreigners, and for whatever distress this stereotyping may have caused them in the context of our multicultural society. (News release, April 16, 1980, CTV Television Network Ltd.)

In 1984 the Chinese in Scarborough, Ontario, were the target of another public debate. Earlier, many Chinese residents and businesses had moved to Scarborough as rising housing prices in Toronto pushed many people to relocate to the suburbs. The apparent increase in the Chinese population caused considerable public outcry. A meeting to discuss the alleged traffic and parking problems caused by the Chinese drew 500 people (*Toronto Star* May 29, 1984), and after it one participant frankly admitted that there was an anti-Chinese sentiment. This racial antagonism prompted the mayor to appoint a task force on Multicultural and Race Relations in Scarborough. These incidents suggest that the Chinese still face substantial obstacles as they try to become permanent citizens of multicultural Canada.

The future of the Chinese in Canada

It is difficult to assess the future prospects for the Chinese in Canada. Undoubtedly the Canadian Charter of Rights and Freedoms provides more protection for the basic individual rights of Canadians. However, notwithstanding the potential contributions of the Charter and the record of human-rights commissions in Canada, there is little guarantee for the collective rights of racial groups. As Kallen (1982: 230) points out, under the Charter 'individual human rights will take precedence over collective (ethnocultural) rights, except in the case of securing the linguistic and religious (cultural) rights of the English and French charter groups.' The Charter is limited in its ability to safeguard social equality. As for human-rights commissions, they spend much of their time handling individual grievances against discrimination, and most of their efforts involve long bureaucratic processes that result, at best, in token compensation for victims. Since the role of human-rights commissions is to mediate between the victim and the offender, they inevitably tend to individualize the problem of racism, thus leaving the structural aspect of racial practices largely untouched (Bolaria and Li, 1985: 29–31).

The future of the Chinese community in Canada also depends on how rapidly its population will increase. Since, until now, the single largest source of increase has been immigration, the future structure of the Chinese-Canadian community depends partly on the kind of immigration policy the government intends to follow. Since 1979 the Canadian immigration policy has placed more emphasis on recruiting business immigrants, especially those with a large amount of capital to invest in Canada. For example, the number of business immigrants increased from 1,237 in 1979 to 2,094 in 1984. Correspondingly, the amount of capital these immigrants brought into Canada jumped from $204 million in 1979 to $817 million in 1984 (Employment and Immigration Canada, 1985). Hong Kong has become a major source supplying Canada with wealthy immigrants; of the total business immigrants admitted in 1984, 41 per cent came from Hong Kong. At the same time, of a total of 3,555 entrepreneurs admitted to Canada in 1984, 52 per cent came from Hong Kong and another 6 per cent from mainland China and Formosa (Taiwan). Many of these new Chinese immigrants have brought substantial wealth into Canada. Some belong to the economic élites of Hong Kong, who control hugh financial empires in the Orient (*Financial Post*, May 11, 1987). Undoubtedly the immigration of these influential Chinese immigrants will exert considerable influence on not only the Chinese community, but also the Canadian financial sector. If the emphasis on recruiting business immigrants is to continue, it can be expected that a new economic élite will emerge among the Chinese in Canada.

9

Race and Culture

Sociological inquiries into racial minorities in North America are often misguided by certain theoretical biases and methodological shortcomings, resulting in many generalizations that are incongruous with historical facts and contemporary realities. These limitations are manifested in a number of popular themes in the literature, such as the transplanted cultural thesis and the assimilation theory. Together with a generally ahistorical approach to sociology, these perspectives tend to confine the kind of research questions being raised to a number of narrowly defined subjects pertaining to immigrant adjustment, cultural adaptation, and ethnic assimilation. This chapter deals with a number of common misconceptions about race and culture, biases that tend to colour the way many Canadians think about racial groups.

Myth and reality of race

One common bias has to do with the unrefined notion of race. It is commonly held that race is based on skin colour, the variations in which connote both genetic and cultural differences. An extreme form of this belief is the view that biological features determine mental and social capacities to such a degree that a racially-based hierarchy expounding white supremacy is both logical and justifiable. There is ample scientific evidence that this view of race is erroneous. In a number of conferences called by the United Nations, experts from around the world have stated some authoritative conclusions on race (Rex, 1983).[1] First, as a concept for classifying human beings, race has limited value because the genetic variation within population groups is as great as that between groups. Second, the only difference between population groups that can be attributed to biological heredity alone is the one related to blood groups; but populations sharing the same blood group do not coincide with racial groups. Third, it is incorrect to attribute cultural characteristics to the effect of genetic inheritance. Fourth, all human groups have the capacity to advance culturally, and this ability overrides the significance of biological or genetic evolution in the evolution of the species. On the basis of these findings Rex (1983: 5) concludes that the term 'race' is a social construct and that, rather than looking into the biological basis of race, it is more meaningful to inquire how people came to be classified as racially different.

Some sociologists have defined race in the context of inter-group relations. Accordingly, physical and cultural traits are able to define social groups only insofar as they are socially recognized as important.[2] In other words, race takes on a social meaning when physical and cultural traits are paired with social attributes, such as intellectual, moral, or behavioural characteristics. Whether such associations are alleged or real is often irrelevant. Attaching a social meaning to the physical or cultural character-istics of a group implies that rewards and resources in society are, to some extent at least, divided along racial lines, and that the dominant group can use the physical and cultural features of people as a basis for stratification.

More recently, Miles (1982) has challenged the use of the term 'race' by social scientists as having the consequence of treating an abstraction as though it were real, or what he calls reification. He argues (1982: 34–5) that if racial groups do not have the same job opportunities, it is not 'race' per se that operates as an active agent affecting job choice. Rather, it is the decision of an employer who refuses to hire someone that determines job opportunity. Accordingly, to claim that race determines oppor-tunity confuses the concept of race with the reality of inequality. In this way race is reified, or treated as though it were a concrete form in the social world.

Limitations of the transplanted cultural thesis

There are many versions of the transplanted cultural thesis. The basic argument is that immigrants to North America bring with them an Old World culture that largely influences their adjust-ment, achievement, and community development in the New World. Over time, as new immigrants take root in North America and become assimilated with the dominant group, their Old World culture begins to weaken. When comparisons are made among racial and ethnic groups, there is a tendency to attribute any differences to cultural variations. Since racial groups are visibly different from European immigrants, their superficial physical traits are often taken to mean that they are culturally more remote from North American society. Consequently, inter-racial differences in behaviour, social status, and achievement are believed to have been caused by the cultural idiosyncracies of the groups being compared.

Athough the transplanted cultural thesis purports to study change, in the sense that there are forces that strengthen or weaken the traditional culture, its approach to culture is mainly static. In this view culture is often seen as primordial and eternal; what is changed is simply immigrants' identity with the traditional culture assumed to have been automatically transplanted with them from their country of origin. This primordial culture is monolithic, and cultural heterogeneity in the home country is rarely considered.

Perhaps the strongest objection to the cultural explanation of racial differences lies in the way the term 'culture' is used. Because it is so all-embracing, it is almost impossible to measure. Conceptually, almost every aspect of human life can be included under the rubric of culture; hence it explains no aspect of human life. Among the strongest critics is Valentine (1968), who points out a potential tautology in using culture as both a description and an explanation. He argues convincingly that there is an important distinction between those material conditions that exist prior to, and therefore apart from, culture, and culture itself. Consequently, disadvantaged racial groups cannot be held responsible for those material conditions that are external to them and over which they have little control. There is also strong historical evidence to indicate that the plight of many racial groups in Canada is the result of structured inequality and racial oppression, and that their subsequent cultural destruction can be directly linked to colonial domination (Frideres, 1983; Milner and Milner, 1973; Bolaria and Li, 1985). In other words, if cultural deprivations and economic failings tend to coexist, it is because they come from the same cause.

In their excellent account of emerging ethnicity in America, Yancey, Ericksen, and Juliani (1976) argue that the development of ethnicity is more related to the structural conditions of American society and the economic opportunities available to each ethnic group than to the primordial culture from the country of origin. Ethnicity and, for that matter, culture are not fixed, but constantly changing under different external conditions. They conclude that 'the assumption of a common heritage as the essential aspect of ethnicity is erroneous', and that 'ethnicity may have relatively little to do with Europe, Asia or Africa, but much to do with the exigencies of survival and the structure of opportunity in this country' (Yancey, Ericksen, and Juliani, 1976: 400).

The assimilationist bias and the multicultural myth

Assimilation is the process whereby people of diverse origins conform to a single or amalgamated culture. This concept has been applied to the study of immigrant groups in North America to see how, over time, they become incorporated into the culture of the dominant group. Assimilation is often equated with Americanization or Anglicization and the upward mobility implied in those terms. Accordingly, if some immigrants are occupying low-status jobs it is because they are not yet assimilated into American society; it is only a question of time until they or their children will enjoy the social advancement that other Americans do now. The social-Darwinian overtone is best illustrated in Park's 'race relation cycle', which describes race relations in successive stages of contact, competition, accommodation, and eventual assimilation (Park, 1950). According to Park this process is progressive and irreversible. Immigration restrictions and racial barriers may slow it down, but they can neither stop nor reverse it.

It is not difficult to see how the assimilationist argument provides a justification for social inequality: the low achievement of some groups is attributed to either their difficulty in assimilating or their unwillingness to do so. In particular, non-white minority groups are easily singled out as non-assimilable because of apparent physical traits and alleged cultural distinctiveness (Li and Bolaria, 1979). The unfounded belief that non-whites are more difficult to assimilate provides an explanation for their economic and social deprivations and a justification for exploitation of coloured labour (Bolaria and Li, 1985).

There are strong theoretical and empirical grounds to suggest that the assimilationist perspective is ethnocentric and limited as a theory (Yancey, Ericksen, and Juliani, 1976). The bias is evident in the three common versions of assimilation theory as outlined by Gordon (1964). The first, Anglo-conformity, is a view of Americanization whereby immigrant groups and racial minorities are to conform to the language, behaviours, and institutions of the dominant Anglo-Saxon group. Anyone who does not conform is therefore non-assimilated. In this respect the perspective echoes the colonial ideology of domination, according to which any behaviours or values of the colonized people that do not conform or converge to the English standard are seen as backward and antithetic to development (see Beckford, 1972). Indigenous societies are believed to be underdeveloped because the so-called traditionalism of the people prevents them from responding to opportunities even when the latter are opened to them. Similarly, racial and ethnic minorities who are limited by what Wagley and Harris (1959) call their 'adaptive capacity'— that is, their cultural readiness to adapt to changing environments—have the least chance to succeed, as in the case of native Indians and blacks.

The second version of assimilation is the melting-pot thesis, according to which all groups are deemed to contribute to the American culture, as people of every stock are amalgamated into a new nation. The irony of the melting-pot concept is that it is difficult to define even for those who are supposed to have been assimilated. The term implies a standard of behaviour and value that immigrant groups have to acquire to be assimilated; yet such a standard is often assumed. For instance, it is often difficult for Canadians to define what a Canadian is, let alone explain to immigrants how to become Canadians. In the absence of an objective criterion of assimilation, any sign of behaviours on the part of immigrants that may suggest adherence to non-English language and culture is often seen as indicating little or no assimilation, no matter how irrelevant these behaviours may be to surviving in North American society. Non-whites and immigrants from Third World countries have the obvious disadvantage of being so-called visible minorities. Their superficial physical traits, such as non-white skin colour, are often paired with assumed values and behaviours that are considered remote from English or American standards. In the minds of the public, these groups will never be considered fully assimilated because they can never become white in colour, no matter how similar their behaviours might become to those of the average Canadian. The notion of the melting-pot remains an idealistic projection of the future, and not an accurate description of ethnic relations in North America.

The third version of assimilation theory, pluralism, stresses both the demise and the persistence of ethnic cultures. It is widely held by Canadians that notions of the melting-pot and assimilation do not apply to Canadian society, which is believed to be pluralistic in culture. No doubt the official policy of multi-culturalism in Canada since 1971 reinforces this belief. In a culturally pluralistic society ethnic groups are believed to share some aspects of a common culture and to participate collectively in its economic and political life, while retaining unique cultural aspects in their social networks, residential enclaves, churches, and languages. Critics argue that pluralists downplay the problem of ethnic and racial inequality and that their view of a plural society often assumes a basic equality for all groups (Steinberg, 1981). Although it is correct to say that groups collectively participate in the same economic and political institutions in North America, the participation is more marginal for some than others, as is evident in the unequal access to politics and social rewards available in the present stratification system. Furthermore, in a society structured on systematic inequality, pluralism can only be an ideal for some ethnic members, as there is no tenable basis for permanent ethnic preservation (Steinberg, 1981). The pluralist perspective has also unduly emphasized the transplanted culture from the old country as the principal antecedent and defining characteristic of ethnic groups (Yancey, Ericksen, and Juliani, 1976). In so doing, cultural pluralists overlook the importance of the structural conditions of the host society in shaping ethnic inequality.

The same criticisms of the pluralist ideal can be applied equally well to Canada's multicultural policy. Made official in 1971, the policy of multiculturalism is to operate within a bilingual framework. Its purpose, as Prime Minister Trudeau put it, is 'to break down discriminatory attitudes and cultural jealousies . . . [and] form the base of a society which is based on fair play for all.' (House of Commons Debates, October 8, 1971: 8545) Despite the intention, there is little indication that racial prejudice has been less prevalent or ethnic inequality less evident. The policy has failed to combat racism and discriminatory practices effectively. Indeed, the persistence of ethnic inequality in the labour market is well documented by the report of the Royal Commission on Equality in Employment (1984). It is also interesting to note that there is no mention of the multicultural policy in the entire report. Judging from how multiculturalism in Canada is implemented, there is clearly a gap between what the multicultural ideal prom- ises and what the institutional reality offers. Most ethnic groups in Canada do not have the structural resources to promote their cultural heritage, and the multicultural policy simply reinforces token or symbolic pluralism (Roberts and Clifton, 1982). For example, with the exception of French, most minority languages are not recognized in the school system as languages of instruc- tion, and multiculturalism operates mainly at the level of folk festivities. As Li and Bolaria (1983: 1) put it, 'the irony of multi- culturalism is that it furnishes Canadian society with a great hope without having to change the fundamental structures of society. Multiculturalism is the failure of an illusion, not of a policy.'

Although the multicultural policy fails to combat racism and discriminatory practices, it succeeds in managing race and ethnic relations within a state apparatus (Bolaria and Li, 1985). The multicultural programs provide an outlet for minorities to organ- ize themselves under state supervision. This is accomplished through fiscal control of ethnic associations whereby the nature, duration, and amount of grants that ethnic associations receive fall in line with the officially defined priorities of multicultural programs. The thrust of these programs is either to encourage ethnic groups to display their cultural heritage, especially those aspects of ethnic food and dance that help to paint a multicultural image of Canada, or to assist individuals in overcoming what are defined as the cultural barriers to their full participation in Cana- dian society (see Stasiulis, 1980). Ethnic associations that do not follow the official priorities run the risk of losing the financial support for their existence. Alternatively, ethnic associations that depend on government funding face the threat of losing organ- izational automomy (Stasiulis, 1980). It is fair to say that the ethnic revival during the seventies in the form of folk festivities and language classes in large part came about because of the funds available through multicultural programs. The ethnic revival was spontaneous to the extent that ethnic groups responded to opportunities of financial support for various 'multicultural' activities.

If the multicultural programs have been limited in their capacity to change race and ethnic relations, it is because they are intended to harmonize, not to resolve social conflicts. It is not difficult to see how multiculturalism as a state policy is appealing to both majority and minority groups. On the one hand, it offers both financial assistance and legitimacy to minority leadership and organizations; on the other, it not only promotes cultural novelties and ethnic entertainments that are not threatening to the livelihood of average Canadians, but also appeals to middle-class Canadians and their Christian ethics by giving them an opportunity to collectively assist needy immigrants to overcome *their* cultural handicaps in adjusting to Canadian life. In this way, as Currie (1982: 63–4) argues, the multicultural policy complements rather than challenges the operations of the labour market by strengthening the belief in equality.

Concluding remarks

The foregoing discussion helps to clarify various myths and distortions regarding race and culture. One of the purposes of this book is to use the case of the Chinese in Canada to present a more realistic picture of racial minorities. Rather than using the cultural origin of the group as a basis for understanding the experiences of the Chinese in Canada, the basic approach here has been to analyze their experiences in the structural context of Canadian society. The conditions under which they first entered Canada and the type of work they performed subsequently can be better explained by taking into account the economic expansion of the Canadian west during the latter half of the nineteenth century. The emergence of institutional racism against the Chinese, in turn, was not based simply on a phobia of a different culture on the part of white Canadians, but was closely related to the conflicting interests of many groups that benefited from the racial exclusion of the Chinese. Subjected to many legal and social constraints, the Chinese in Canada before the war were forced to adapt to a hostile environment that offered them limited options. The development of various ethnic institutions under these conditions, therefore, has to be seen in a larger societal context, and not simply as an extension of a transplanted culture. Similarly, the post-war changes among the Chinese community were influenced by the changing economic conditions and immigration policies in Canada, and were not necessarily a result of the Chinese becoming more assimilated into Canadian society. Likewise, the apparent occupational and educational mobility of the post-war Chinese has had more to do with the overall shifts in the occupational structure in Canada than with greater equality for racial minorities.

Emphasis on concrete historical conditions provides a solid background for understanding the contemporary situation of the Chinese in Canada. In tracing the structural relationships that affect the life and organization of the Chinese community, this book does not stress the cultural aspect of race relations. As Bolaria and Li (1985: 1) put it, 'if one insists that racial groups are cultural groups, then one is not likely to uncover the economic basis of racial exploitation, for such a relationship falls outside the parameter of a cultural framework.'

The future of Chinese-Canadians depends in part on the kind of policies toward racial minorities that Canada intends to follow. For the past two decades, the single largest source of population increase in the Chinese-Canadian community has been the change in immigration policy, which has enabled a larger volume of Chinese immigrants to enter. That policy also determines the kind of Chinese who can become future Canadians. It is not clear what changes in immigration policy are forthcoming. By the same token, it is not evident whether the Canadian government plans to change its multicultural policy to one that would produce more racial equity, or to simply follow the present course of action, or inaction. From a sociological point of view the treatment of racial minorities, and their responses to it, are parts of the same reality and therefore cannot be understood in isolation from each other. Although this book is a case study of the Chinese, it has much larger implications for Canadian society. Policies on racial minorities frequently reflect more the internal contradictions of the state that engineers them than the groups to which the policies are supposedly applied. These policies in turn are determined by other social forces, not the least of which are the changing labour needs Canada will face in the future as it is transformed by an advanced technology and an aging population.

Notes

Introduction

[1] The blacks did not become slaves because of their skin colour but were recruited as slaves because of the shortage of labour. Once they became slaves, their skin colour provided convenient grounds for legitimation. As Cox (1948: 332) put it, the slave trade 'did not develop because Indians and Negroes were red and black . . . but because they were the best workers to be found for the heavy labour in the mines and plantations across the Atlantic.'

[2] Rosen (1956, 1959) further breaks down the achievement syndrome into three components: achievement motivation, value orientation, and educational-vocational aspiration.

[3] For a critique of status-attainment models see Horan (1978) and Kerkoff (1976).

[4] For a theoretical alternative to status-attainment models using class analysis see Wright (1977, 1978, 1979).

1: Chinese Emigration

[1] There have been suggestions that a Chinese monk named Hwui-Shan may have visited Canada as early as A.D. 499 (Lee, 1967: 27). Morton (1974: 5) suggests that the first group of Chinese to attempt to come to British North America were thirty artisans brought by Captain John Meares in 1779, but after the ship was seized by the Spanish their fate is unknown.

[2] These are estimates based on the number of Chinese passengers in vessels entering the port of Victoria. See Royal Commission (1885: 397–9).

[3] *1890 U.S. Census, Population and Social Statistics*, vol. I, table XXII, p. 613 (Statistics of the Population of the United States, 1890).

[4] The Chinese Six Companies were the predecessors of the Chinese Consolidated Benevolent Association, which is still active in most Chinatowns in cities throughout North America. In 1876 the six companies were estimated to control 148,600 Chinese. The original six companies and the number of Chinese belonging to them in 1876 were as follows: Yam Yup, 10,100; Yung Wo, 10,200; Kong Chow, 15,000; Wing Young, 75,000; Yan Wo, 4,300; Hop Wo, 34,000 (Senate of California, Committee on Chinese Immigration, 1876: 44). Since the 1880 U.S. Census reported only 105,465 Chinese (Statistics of the Population of the United States, 1880: Table XIX, pp. 544–5), it is reasonable to assume that most of the Chinese in the 1870s were under the

Chinese Six Companies. For a discussion of the Chinese Six Companies and their role in contract labour see the *Report of the Joint Special
Committee to Investigate Chinese Immigration* (U.S. Congress, 1877),
especially pp. 23–4, 34–50, 82–5, 111–14, 405–6, 446–8.

5 Fifteen *mu* (*mou*) is equal to one hectare.

6 In the province of Guangdong (Kwangtung), for example, 70 per cent
of all farm families in 1888 were tenants (Perkins, 1969: 101).

7 The edict that prohibited Chinese emigration became ineffective after
1842 and was rescinded in 1893 (Liu and Shu, 1971).

8 The English translation of the name is not consistent. Taishan (T'ai-
shan) is also known as Toy-shan and Toishan, while San-ning is sometimes spelled as Sining or Sing-ning.

9 The figure is based on a 10 per cent random sample (Public Archives
of Canada, *General Register of Chinese Immigration, 1885–1903*, Record
Group 76, vols. 694–703).

10 According to Irick (1982: 2–3), the term 'coolie' does not come from
the Chinese term *k'u-li*, as some authors mistakenly assume (e.g.
Chan, 1983: 39). *K'u-li* means 'bitter labour', whereas coolie is an
Indian term 'adopted by foreigners to describe menial labourers in
China as well as India' (Irick, 1982: 4).

2: Racism Against The Chinese

1 Exempted from the head tax were diplomats, tourists, merchants, and
students. Merchants were exempted because of the concern that their
exclusion would jeopardize trade with China. Between 1874 and 1884
the value of goods imported from China to Canada amounted to $1.4
million. For the same period the total duty received by the Canadian
government was $411,970.60, half of which was collected in 1883 and
1884 (Royal Commission, 1885: iv).

2 The Chinese and Japanese were the only groups singled out in the
1931 order-in-council, which required them to obtain consent from
their country of origin prior to apply for Canadian citizenship; This
order was revoked in 1947 (Privy Council 1947–567).

3 The 1914 Naturalization Act applied to all, not just the Chinese.

4 For examples see Statutes of British Columbia 1884, c. 3; Statutes of
British Columbia 1885, c. 13; Canadian Reports, Appeal Cases, 1899:
vol. 12 (*Union Colliery Company* v. Bryden), 580.

5 The government of Canada did not want the Chinese Immigration Act
to jeopardize international trade between China and Canada, and the
inclusion of Chinese 'merchants' as an admissible category of entry
was intended to facilitate future trade. See Canada House of Commons
Debates, 1923: vol. III, p. 2311.

6 The value of the head tax becomes more apparent when it is compared to the cost of other items at that time. For example, the weekly cost to an average family in British Columbia of staple foods, fuel, lighting, and rent in the month of December, for 1900–20 was as follows:

	1900	1905	1910	1920
Staple foods	$6.90	$7.74	$9.06	$15.93
Fuel and lighting	1.86	1.73	2.20	3.75
Rent	3.26	3.78	4.64	6.38
Total	12.02	13.25	15.90	26.06

Source: *Canada Year Book*, 1921, table 30, p. 650.

7 Calculations of the excise duties and the defense budget are based on the *Historical Statistics of Canada*, tables H1–18, and H19–34 (Statistics Canada, 1983).

3: Occupations and Ethnic Business

1 The split labour market refers to the price differentials between two groups performing the same task, or in a submerged form in which the higher-paid group monopolizes certain positions and the lower-paid group is restricted to marginal participation (Bonacich, 1972, 1979).

2 The fact that unions frequently blamed the Chinese for depressing wages is itself an indication of the fact that differential wage scales existed.

3 Although evidence in Canada is lacking, Saxton (1971) provides detailed discussions regarding the social organization in gold fields in the United States. Chinese were often hired as cooks, servants, and firewood collectors, and some managed to become independent miners only in low-quality surface claims abandoned by white miners (Saxton, 1971: 52–7). Li (1978: 40) also suggests that anti-Chinese agitation in the United States was frequently aimed not so much at excluding the Chinese physically from mines as at excluding them from the right to mine.

4 For a good summary of workers' complaints against the Chinese, see the briefs submitted by Knights of Labour L.A. No. 3017, Nanaimo, B.C. to the Royal Commission on Chinese Immigration (1885: 155–60). With regard to the validity of these allegations, one author comments, 'After having made an intensive examination of the relevant materials, one is inclined to believe that labourites exaggerated the evils resulting from their presence' (Saywell, 1951: 133).

5 Although the 1885 figures apply to Chinese in British Columbia, 98

per cent of all Chinese in Canada at that time in fact resided in the province (Dept. of Agriculture, 1893: 133–4).

[6] According to the 1901 Census of Canada, 86 per cent of all Chinese in Canada resided in British Columbia and about 20 per cent of those in Victoria (Statistics Canada, 1902: vol. 1, *Population*, table xii, pp. 406–7).

4: Marriage and the Family

[1] Among the 76 families were 92 wives and 145 children. Assuming that there were 76 adult males, the average size per family would be (76 + 92 + 145) divided by 76 = 4.1 (Royal Commission, 1902: 13).

[2] The evidence on the American-Chinese family during the same period suggests an almost identical pattern under similar legislative controls before the war (see Lyman, 1977; Nee and Nee, 1973; Siu 1953).

[3] Testimonies before the 1902 Royal Commission suggested that mixed marriages were unlikely. Of the 109 babies born to Chinese mothers in 1936, 108 had Chinese fathers and one a white father. In addition there were 5 babies with Chinese fathers and white mothers (Woodsworth, 1941: 144).

5: Community Organizations and Social Life

[1] Although patrilineage influenced various levels of familial organization in southeastern China (Freedman, 1958), its effect on the Chinese community in Canada was almost non-existent (Willmott, 1964).

[2] The Zhi Gong Tang (Chih-kung T'ang) was a branch of the Hongmen (Hung-men), or Hong Society, another name for the Triad Society (Lyman, 1970: 152; Con, et al., 1982: 30); after the Second World War its members were referred to as the Chinese Freemasons, although they bore little relation to the Freemasons of the west other than maintaining a degree of secrecy.

[3] In 1911, for example, the Zhi Gong Tang of Victoria mortgaged its building to raise funds to support the revolution in China led by Sun Yat-sen (Lee, 1967: 242–3).

[4] These rules were translated and originally published in Lyman, Willmott, and Ho (1964), and later reprinted in Lyman (1970).

[5] Willmott (1964) suggests using five categories to classify the Chinese associations in Canada: clan associations based on common surnames, locality associations based on home counties, fraternal associations such as the Zhi Gong Tang, community associations such as the Chinese Benevolent Association, and a residual category of other associations.

[6] Before the Second World War the English names commonly used for

this association in many Chinese communities were the Chinese Benevolent Association and the Chinese Consolidated Benevolent Association, or CBA. After the war some of these associations changed their names to Chinese Community Centre (Lee, 1967: 198–202).

7 There is evidence to suggest that Chinese merchants and workers had different class interests despite a general discrimination against the Chinese. For example, when the Chinese workers staged a general strike in Victoria in 1878 to protest against a discriminatory tax, the Chinese merchants publicly dissociated themselves from the strikers (Sedgwick and Willmott, 1974).

8 For a discussion of the reform movement and the subsequent coup d'état in China in 1898 see the *Chronological Autobiography of Kan Youwei* (K'ang Yu-wei), edited and translated by Lo (1967), especially pp. 83–144.

9 Opium smoking was not illegal in Canada until the enactment of the Opium Act of 1908. Comack (1986: 86) argues that 'the drug legislation was not so much directed at the Chinese but rather helped to identify them as a major source of the problems confronting B.C. society.' There is also evidence to indicate that both the federal and provincial governments collected substantial revenue from the opium trade, which peaked between 1885 and 1895 (Comack, 1986).

6: Chinese Immigration to Canada

1 A document entitled *Oriental Canadians: Outcasts or Citizens*, written by Grace and Angus MacInnis, outlined the position of the Cooperative Commonwealth Federation on the oriental question. It was probably written between 1944 and 1945.

2 This is the abbreviation for Privy Council, number 2115, issued in 1930. The same system of abbreviation is used in this book for all orders-in-council.

3 The 1930 order-in-council included a clause stating 'that this regulation shall not apply to the nationals of any country in regard to which there is in operation a law . . . regulating immigration' (P.C. 1930–2115). As a result of the Chinese Immigration Act of 1923, therefore, the Chinese were not covered by this order-in-council before 1947.

4 The 1931 order-in-council (P.C. 1931–1378) required that Chinese applying for Canadian citizenship obtain consent from the Ministry of the Interior in China. The Chinese were the only ones in Canada to have to obtain consent from the ministry of a foreign country as a condition for Canadian citizenship.

5 Immigrants from India, Pakistan, and Ceylon were admitted under annual quotas of 150, 100, and 50 respectively, as a result of an agreement between Canada and these countries (P.C. 1956–785).

6 The Chinese in the U.S. also responded to restrictive immigration measures by using fictive kinship to circumvent the immigration law. For a discussion of the restrictive immigration laws against the Chinese between 1882 and 1971, and the response mechanisms developed by the Chinese using real and fictive kinship, see Li (1977).

7 This clause is under Immigration Regulations, Part I, section 31 (d), P.C. 1962–86 (*Canada Gazette* Part II, vol. 96, Feb. 14, 1962, pp. 138–9).

8 Largely under the influence of the United States, Canada participated in the United Nations army against China in the Korean war (1950–53). There was no formal diplomatic relationship between Canada and China until 1971.

9 Table 4.2 shows that the percentage of Canadian-born Chinese was 38 per cent in 1971 and 25 per cent in 1981. The lower figure in 1981 was accounted for by a larger volume of Chinese immigrating between 1971 and 1981. As more foreign-born Chinese entered Canada, they tended to increase the foreign-born population in the Chinese community. In absolute terms, however, there were 72,311 Canadian-born Chinese in 1981, as compared with 45,149 in 1971.

7: Contemporary Chinese-Canadians

1 The figure of 285,800 was calculated from the Individual File, Public Use Sample Tape, Census of Canada 1981. The Individual File is based on 2 per cent sample of the total population. In Table 4.2 it is reported that there were 289,245 Chinese in 1981. This number is obtained from 1981 Census of Canada, *A User's Guide to 1981 Census Data on Ethnic Origin*, table 8, pp. 32–6.

2 On January 27, 1980, 1,500 demonstrators, mostly Chinese, rallied in Toronto against a CTV program that depicted Chinese students as foreign students taking away university openings from qualified Canadians (*Globe and Mail*, Jan. 28, 1980). A movement to advance greater equality for Chinese-Canadians grew from this incident.

3 The index of segregation measures the percentage of an ethnic group that would have to be moved if there were no residential segregation. The index has a value that ranges from 0 to 100. The higher the index value, the greater the residential segregation for that group relative to another.

4 The actual number of Chinese cultural organizations is likely to be higher, given that only head offices were counted in the tabulation, and organizations that did not advise the Secretary of State were not included.

5 In the sociological literature the problem of language loss is measured in two ways: ancestral shift and current shift. The difference between the number of people in an ethnic origin and the number of people

maintaining the same mother tongue measures the ancestral shift, or the shift that occurred in previous generations. The difference between the number of people claiming a common mother tongue and the number of people speaking the same language at home measures the current shift, or the shift that occurs in the current generation (de Vries and Vallee, 1980: 101–33).

[6] The secondary family refers to any census family in which a person responsible for household payments is not a member (Census of Canada, *Census Dictionary*, 1981: 62).

8: Social Mobility and Inequality

[1] The 'working age' is defined differently in various census years. For 1911 and all previous censuses it includes those ten years of age and over; for 1921, fourteen and over; and for 1961 and later censuses, fifteen years and over.

[2] The real domestic product by industry is a way of showing the industrial composition of changes in the physical volume of output. It 'portrays the pattern of industry advances and declines, behind the increases and declines in total real output' (Statistics Canada, 1983: F221–94).

[3] Calculations based on constant values take into account changes due to inflation. Using this index, the value for 1971 is 100.

[4] The economic return of schooling can be estimated using the regression model: $Y = a + bX$, where Y = annual earning; X = years of schooling; a = intercept; and b = slope, or regression coefficient. Estimating a separate regression for each ethnic group, the differences in slopes show the differential return for each unit increase in schooling. The regression coefficient for Jewish origin is 1299.97; for British, 1104.35; for Chinese, 955.79; and for black, 933.97. The calculations are based on the 1981 Census of Canada, Public Use Sample Tape, Individual File.

[5] It follows that if the value is equal to or close to the mean, it suggests that membership in the given ethnic origin has no impact on the annual earnings.

[6] The gross and net effects of ethnic origin are calculated using Multiple Classification Analysis (Andrews, et al. 1976), in which income differences between groups are measured as deviations from the grand mean such that the weighted sum is equal to zero. The net effects measure the impact of ethnic origin on earnings when differences in other variables have been adjusted for.

[7] There were many inaccuracies in the report. In a letter to the CTV network dated October 18, 1979, Mr. James R. McBride, Executive Director of the Canadian Bureau for International Education, pointed

out that there were only 55,000 foreign students in Canada at all levels of education and that, contrary to the report, there was not a single foreign student in the Faculty of Pharmacy at the University of Toronto.

9: Race and Culture

[1] These conclusions are incorporated in the Moscow Declaration of 1964, cited in Rex (1983).
[2] For example, in South Africa every person is legally defined in a racial category. However, a person may have fair skin and still can be classified as black because one of his or her parents is legally black. This shows that there is no direct correspondence among skin colour, genetical grouping, and social classification.

References

Public documents

CANADA

British Columbia Fisheries Commission
  1922   *Report and Recommendations.*
Canadian Reports, Appeal Cases
  1899   *Union Company versus Bryden.* Vol. 12, 580.
  1903   *Cunningham versus Tomey Homma.* Vol. 13, 151.
Department of Agriculture
  1886   *Statistical Abstracts and Records Canada.* Ottawa.
  1893   *The Statistical Yearbook of Canada.* Ottawa.
Department of Citizenship and Immigration
  1950   *Annual Report of the Department of Citizenship and Immigration.*
          Ottawa.
Department of Mines and Resources
  1947-   *Report of the Department of Mines and Resources, Immigration*
  1948   *Branch.* Ottawa.
Employment and Immigration Canada
  1982   *Indochinese Refugees: The Canadian Response, 1979 and 1980.*
          Ottawa.
  1985   *Business Immigrants.* Ottawa.
House of Commons
  1883   *Debates, 1st Session, 5th Parliament*
  1923   *Debates, 2nd Session, 14th Parliament*
  1960   *Debates, 3rd Session, 24th Parliament*
  1971   *Debates, 3rd Session, 28th Parliament*
Public Archives of Canada
  1885-   'General register of Chinese immigration.' Record Group A-1,
  1903   Vol. 694-703.
  1886   'Destitute conditions of Chinese labourers discharged from
          CPR.' Record Group A-l, Vol. 60, File 2235.
Royal Commission
  1885   *Report of the Royal Commission on Chinese Immigration: Report*
          and Evidence.
  1902   *Report of the Royal Commission on Chinese and Japanese*
          Immigration.
  1907   *Report of the Royal Commission on the Losses Sustained By The*
          Chinese Population of Vancouver, B.C. on the Occasion of the Riots
          in that City in September, 1907.
  1984   *Report of the Commission on Equality in Employment.*
Sessional Paper
  1909   *First Session of the Eleventh Parliament.* Vol. 17, no. 36.

Special Committee on Orientals in B.C.
  1940   *Report and Recommendations*. Public Archives of Canada,
          Record Group 27, Vol. 1500, File 2-k-184.
Statistics Canada
  1902   *Census of Canada, 1901, Population*. Vol. 1.
  1936   *Census of Canada, 1931, Occupations and Industries*. Vol. VII.
  1941   *Census of Canada, 1941, General Review and Summary Tables*.
  1974   *Perspective Canada: A Compendium of Social Statistics*.
  1981a *Population, Ethnic Origin*. Vol. I.
  1981b *Census of Canada, Public Use Sample Tape, Individual File*.
  1983   *Historical Statistics of Canada*, 2d ed.
Statutes of British Columbia
  1875   An Act relating to an Act to make better provision for the
          Qualification and Registration of Voters. No. 2.
  1884   An Act to prevent Chinese from acquiring Crown Lands. C. 2.
            1884   An Act to prevent the Immigration of Chinese. C. 3.
  1885   An Act to prevent the Immigration of Chinese. C. 13.
  1890   Coal Mines Regulation Amendment Act. C. 33.
  1893   An Act to provide for the establishment and maintenance of a
          Provincial Home for the Aged and Infirm. C. 35.
  1895   Provincial Voters' Act Amendment. C. 20.
  1896   An Act to consolidate and amend the law relating to Electors
          and Elections in Municipalities. C. 38.
  1897   An Act relating to the employment of Chinese or Japanese
          persons on Works carried on under Franchises granted by
          Private Acts. C. 1.
  1899   An Act Respecting Liquor Licences. C. 39.
  1903   Coal Mines Regulation Act Further Amendment Act. C. 17.
  1917   Civil Service Act. C. 9.
  1920   Provincial Elections Act. C. 27.
  1922   Factories Act Amendment Act, 1922. C. 25.
  1923   Women's and Girls' Protection Act. C. 76.
Statues of Canada
  1885   An Act to restrict and regulate Chinese Immigration into
          Canada. C. 71.
  1900   An Act respecting and restricting Chinese Immigration. C.
          32.
  1903   An Act respecting and restricting Chinese Immigration. C. 8.
  1914   An Act respecting British Nationality, Naturalization and
          Aliens. C. 44.
  1917   The War-time Elections Act. C. 39.
  1920   The Dominion Elections Act. C. 46.
  1923   An Act respecting Chinese Immigration. C. 38.
  1929   The Dominion Elections Act Amendment Act. C. 40.

1947   An Act to amend the Immigration Act and to repeal the
        Chinese Immigration Act. C. 19.
Statutes of Ontario
1914   An Act to Amend the Factory, Shop and Office Building Act.
        C. 40.
Statutes of Saskatchewan
1908   An Act respecting Elections of Members of the Legislative
        Assembly. C. 2.
1912   An Act to Prevent the Employment of Female Labour in
        Certain Capacities. C. 17.
Supreme Court of Canada
1914   *Quong-Wing* v. *The King*. Reports of the Supreme Court of
        Canada. Vol. 49, 441.

U.S.

Senate of California, Committee on Chinese Immigration
1876   *Chinese Immigration: The Social, Moral, and Political Effect of
        Chinese Immigration*. Sacramento: State Printing Office.
Statistics of the Population of the United States
1880   *United States Census.*
1890   *United States Census, Population and Social Statistics*. Vol. 1.
U.S. Congress, Committee to Investigate Chinese Immigration
1877   *Report of the Joint Special Committee to Investigate Chinese
        Immigration*. Washington: Government Printing Office.

Books and Articles

Adachi, Ken
1976   *The Enemy That Never Was: A History of the Japanese Canadians.*
        Toronto: McClelland and Stewart.
Andrews, Frank M., James N. Morgan, John A. Sonquist, and Laura
Klem
1976   *Multiple Classification Analysis*. Ann Arbor: Institute For Social
        Research, Univ. of Michigan.
Angus, H. F.
1937   'Canadian immigration: the law and its administration.'
        Pp. 58-75 in Norman Mackenzie, ed. *The Legal Status of Aliens
        in Pacific Countries*. London: Oxford Univ. Press.
Ashworth, Mary
1979   *The Forces Which Shaped Them: A History of the Education of
        Minority Group Children in British Columbia*. Vancouver: New
        Star Books.

Auster, Ellen, and Howard Aldrich
  1984   'Small business vulnerability, ethnic enclaves and ethnic
          enterprise.' Pp. 39-54 in Robin Ward and Richard Jenkins,
          eds. *Ethnic Communities in Business*. Cambridge: Cambridge
          Univ. Press.
Bancroft, Hubert Howe
  1890   *The Works of Hubert Howe Bancroft*. Vol. XXIV, *History of
          California*. Vol. VII, 1860-1890. San Francisco: The History
          Company.
Beckford, George L.
  1972   *Persistent Poverty: Underdevelopment in Plantation Economies of
          the Third World*. New York: Oxford Univ. Press.
Berry, John W., Rudolf Kalin, and Donald M. Taylor
  1977   *Multiculturalism and Ethnic Attitudes in Canada*. Ottawa:
          Minister of Supply and Services Canada.
Blau, Peter, and Otis D. Duncan
  1967   *The American Occupation Structure*. New York: John Wiley.
Blauner, Robert
  1972   *Racial Oppression in America*. New York: Harper & Row.
Bolaria, B. Singh, and Peter S. Li
  1985   *Racial Oppression in Canada*. Toronto: Garamond.
Bonacich, Edna
  1972   'A theory of ethnic antagonism: the split labour market.'
          American Sociological Review 37: 547-59.
  1975   'Abolition, the extension of slavery, and the position of free
          blacks: a study of split labour markets in the United States,
          1830-1836.' *American Journal of Sociology* 81: 601-28.
  1976   'Advanced capitalism and black/white race relations in the
          United States: a split labour market interpretation.' *American
          Sociological Review* 41: 34-51.
  1979   'The past, present, and future of split labor market theory.'
          Pp. 17-64 in C.B. Marrett and C. Leggon, eds. *Research in Race
          and Ethnic Relations*. Vol. 1. Greenwich, Conn.: JAI Press.
Bonacich, Edna, and John Modell
  1980   *The Economic Basis of Ethnic Solidarity*. Berkeley: Univ. of
          California Press.
Boyd, Monica, John Goyder, Frank E. Jones, Hugh A. McRoberts,
  Peter C. Pineo, John Porter
  1985   *Ascription and Achievement: Studies in Mobility and Status
          Attainment in Canada*. Ottawa: Carleton Univ. Press.
Campbell, Persia C.
  1969   *Chinese Coolie Emigration*. New York: Negro Univ. Press.
Chan, Anthony B.
  1983   *Gold Mountain*. Vancouver: New Star Books.

Chen Hansheng
  1981   *Huagong chuguo shiliao* (Historical Materials on Emigration of
         Chinese Workers). Vol. 4. Beijing, China: Zhonghua shuju.
Cheng Tien-Fang
  1931   *Oriental Immigration in Canada.* Shanghai, China: The
         Commercial Press.
Chow, W.S.
  1976   'The Chinese community in Canada before 1947 and some
         recent developments.' Pp. 115-35 in Frances Henry, ed.
         Ethnicity in Americas. The Hague, Netherlands: Mouton
         Publishers.
Comack, Elizabeth
  1986   ' "We will get some good out of this riot yet": the Canadian
         state, drug legislation and class conflict.' Pp. 67-89 in Stephen
         Brickey and Elizabeth Comack, eds. *The Social Basis of Law:
         Critical Readings in the Sociology of Law.* Toronto: Garamond.
Con, Harry, Ronald J. Con, Graham Johnson, Edgar Wickberg,
  William E. Willmott
  1982   *From China to Canada: A History of the Chinese Communities in
         Canada.* Toronto: McClelland and Stewart.
Connelly, M.P.
  1976   'Canadian Women as a Reserve Army of Labour.' Ph.D. diss.,
         Ontario Institute for Studies in Education, Univ. of Toronto.
Cox, Oliver C.
  1948   *Caste, Class & Race: A Study in Social Dynamics.* New York:
         Doubleday and Co.
Cuneo, Carl, and James Curtis
  1975   'Social ascription in the education and occupational status
         attainment of urban Canadians.' *Canadian Review of Sociology
         and Anthropology* 12: 6-24.
Currie, D.H.
  1982   'Multiculturalism and Inequality: A Study of the Voluntary
         Agency.' Unpublished M.A. research report. Depart. of
         Sociology, Univ. of Saskatchewan.
deVries, John, and Frank G. Vallee
  1980   *Language Use in Canada.* 1971 Census of Canada, Catalogue
         99-762E. Ottawa: Statistics Canada.
Duncan, Beverly, and Otis Dudley Duncan
  1968   'Minorities and the process of stratification.' *American
         Sociological Review* 33: 356-64.
Featherman, David L.
  1971   'The socioeconomic achievement of white religio-ethnic
         subgroups: social and psychological explanations.' *American
         Sociological Review* 36: 207-22.

Fei Hsiao-Tung
   1946   'Peasantry and gentry: an interpretation of Chinese social
           structure and its changes.' *American Journal of Sociology* 52: 1-
           17.
Financial Post
   1987   'Hong Kong family firms paved the way.' May 11.
Freedman, Maurice
   1958   'Lineage organization in South-eastern China.' *L.S.E.
           Monographs on Social Anthropology* 18. London: Athlone Press.
   1961– 'The family in China, past and present.' *Pacific Affairs* 24:
   1962   323-36.
Frideres, James S.
   1983   *Native People in Canada: Contemporary Conflicts*. 2d ed.
           Scarborough, Ont.: Prentice-Hall.
Genovese, Eugene D.
   1967   *The Political Economy of Slavery*. New York: Vintage.
Globe and Mail, The
   1980   '1,500 march to protest CTV program.' Jan. 28.
Gordon, Milton M.
   1964   *Assimilation in American Life: The Role of Race, Religion, and
           National Origins*. New York: Oxford Univ. Press.
Green, Alan G.
   1976   *Immigration and the Postwar Canadian Economy*. Toronto:
           Macmillan of Canada.
Greene, Felix
   1971   *The Enemy*. New York: Vintage.
Hauser, Phillip M. and David L. Featherman
   1977   *The Process of Stratification*. New York: Academic Press.
Hawkins, Freda
   1972   *Canada and Immigration: Public Policy and Public Concern* .
           Montreal: McGill-Queen's Univ. Press
Ho Ping-ti
   1965   'A historian's view of the Chinese family system.' Pp. 15-28
           in S.M. Farber, P. Mustacchi, and R.H.L. Wilson, eds. *Man
           and Civilization: The Family's Search for Survival*. New York:
           McGraw-Hill.
   1967   *Studies on the Population of China, 1368-1953*. Cambridge,
           Mass.: Harvard Univ. Press.
Hoe Ban Seng
   1976   *Structural Changes of Two Chinese Communities in Alberta,
           Canada*. Mercury Series, CCFCS Paper No. 19. Ottawa:
           National Museums of Canada.
Horan, Patrick M.
   1978   'Is status attainment research atheoretical?' *American
           Sociological Review* 43: 534-41.

References | 149

Hsu, Immanuel C. Y.
  1970   *The Rise of Modern China*. New York: Oxford Univ. Press.
Hughes, David R., and Evelyn Kallen
  1974   *The Anatomy of Racism: Canadian Dimensions*. Montreal:
         Harvest House.
Ireland, Ralph R.
  1960   'Some effects of oriental immigration on Canadian trade
         union ideology.' *American Journal of Economics and Sociology* 19:
         217-20
Irick, Robert L.
  1982   *Ch'ing Policy Toward the Coolie Trade, 1847-1878*. China:
         Chinese Materials Center.
Jencks, Christopher, et al.
  1972   *Inequality: A Reassessment of the Effect of Family and Schooling in
         America*. New York: Harper Colophon.
Kallen, Evelyn
  1982   *Ethnicity and Human Rights in Canada*. Toronto: Gage.
Kerckhoff, Alan C.
  1976   'The status attainment process: socialization or allocation?'
         Social Forces 55: 368-81.
Kung, S.W.
  1961- 'Chinese immigration into North America with special
  1962   reference to the problem of illegal entry.' *Queen's Quarterly* 68:
         610-20.
Lai, Chuen-Yan David
  1972   'The Chinese Consolidated Benevolent Association in
         Victoria: its origins and functions.' *BC Studies* 15: 53-67.
  1973   'Chinese attempts to discourage emigration to Canada: Some
         findings from the Chinese archives in Victoria.' *BC Studies* 18:
         33-49.
  1975   Home country and clan origins of overseas Chinese in
         Canada in the early 1800s.' *BC Studies* 27: 3-29.
  1980   'The population structure of North American Chinatowns in
         the mid-twentieth century: a case study.' Pp. 13-21 in K.
         Victor Ujimoto and Gordon Hirabayashi, eds. *Visible
         Minorities and Multiculturalism: Asians in Canada*. Toronto:
         Butterworths.
Lamb, Kaye W.
  1977   *History of Canadian Pacific Railway*. New York: Macmillan.
Lee, Carol F.
  1976   'The road to enfranchisement: Chinese and Japanese in
         British Columbia.' *BC Studies* 30: 44-76.
Lee Tung-hai
  1967   *Jianada Huaqiao Shi* (History of Overseas Chinese in Canada).
         Taipei, Taiwan.

Levy, Marion J. Jr.
Lewis, Oscar
  1959   *Five Families: Mexican Case Studies in the Culture of Poverty*.
          New York: Basic.
  1964   'The culture of poverty.' Pp. 149-73 in J. Tepaske and S.
          Fisher, eds. *Explosive Forces in Latin America*. Ohio Univ. Press.
  1966a   *La Vida: A Puerto Rican Family in the Culture of Poverty — San
          Juan and New York*. New York: Random House.
  1966b   'The culture of poverty.' *Scientific American* 215: 19-25.
  1963   *The Family Revolution in Modern China*. New York: Octagon.
Li, Peter S.
  1976   'Ethnic businesses among Chinese in the U.S.' *Journal of
          Ethnic Studies* 4: 35-41.
  1977   'Fictive kinship, conjugal tie and kinship chain among
          Chinese immigrants in the United States.' *Journal of
          Comparative Family Studies* 8: 47-63.
  1978   *Occupational Mobility and Kinship Assistance: A Study of Chinese
          Immigrants in Chicago*. San Francisco: R & E Research
          Associates.
  1979a   'A historical approach to ethnic stratification: the case of the
          Chinese in Canada, 1858-1930.' *Canadian Review of Sociology
          and Anthropology* 16: 320-32.
  1979b   'Prejudice against Asians in a Canadian city.' *Canadian Ethnic
          Studies* 11: 70-7.
  1980a   'Immigration laws and family patterns: some demographic
          changes among Chinese in Canada.' *Canadian Ethnic Studies*
          12: 58-73.
  1980b   'Income achievement and adaptive capacity: an empirical
          comparison of Chinese and Japanese in Canada.' Pp. 363-78
          in K. Victor Ujimoto and Gordon Hirabayashi, eds. *Visible
          Minorities and Multiculturalism: Asians in Canada*. Scarborough,
          Ont.: Butterworths.
  1982   'Chinese immigrants on the Canadian prairie, 1910-47.'
          Canadian Review of Sociology and Anthropology 19: 527-40.
  1983a   'Minority business and ethnic neighbourhood: some
          observations on Chinese-owned firms in Vancouver.' Paper
          presented at the annual meeting of the Canadian Sociology
          and Anthropology Association, June 1-4, Univ. of British
          Columbia.
  1983b   'Marriage and minority families.' Pp. 86-96 in Peter S. Li and
          B. Singh Bolaria, eds. *Racial Minorities in Multicultural Canada*.
          Toronto: Garamond.
  1985   'The use of oral history in studying elderly Chinese-
          Canadians.' *Canadian Ethnic Studies* 17: 67-77.
Li, Peter S., and B. Singh Bolaria

1979 'Canadian immigration policy and assimilation theories.'
Pp. 411-22 in John A. Fry, ed. *Economy, Class and Social Reality*.
Scarborough, Ont.: Butterworths.

1983 *Racial Minorities in Multicultural Canada*. Toronto: Garamond.

Light, Ivan, and Charles Choy Wong

1975 'Protest or work: dilemmas of the tourist industry in American
Chinatowns.' *American Journal of Sociology* 80: 1342-68.

Lipset, Seymour M., and Reinhard Bendix

1966 *Social Mobility and Industrial Society*. Berkeley: Univ. of
California Press.

Liu Chi-Hsuan, and Shih-Cheng Shu

1971 *Zhonghua minzu tuozhi Nanyang shi*. (The History of
Emigration of Chinese to Southeast Asia). Reprint of 1934
edition. Taipei: Commercial Press.

Liu Yuzun, Lucie Cheng Hirata, and Zheng Dehua

1980 'Overseas Chinese, the Xinning Railroad and Taishan
County.' *Journal of Sun Yat-sen University* 4: 24-47.

Lo Jung-Pang, ed. and trans.

1967 *K'ang Yu-wei*: A Biography and a Symposium. Tucson:
Univ. of Arizona Press.

Lyman, Stanford M.

1970 *The Asian in the West*. Nevada: Desert Research Institute,
Univ. of Nevada System.

1977 *The Asian in North America*. California: ABC-Clio, Inc.

Lyman, Stanford M., W.E. Willmott, and Berching Ho.

1964 'Rules of a Chinese secret society in British Columbia.'
Bulletin of the School of Oriental and African Studies 27: 530-9.

MacInnis, Grace, and Angus MacInnis

n.d. 'Oriental Canadians: Outcasts or Citizens.' n.p.

MacNair, Harley F.

1927 *Modern Chinese History: Selected Readings*. Vol. I. Shanghai,
China: Commerical Press.

McRoberts, Hugh A., and Kevin Selbee

1981 'Trends in occupational mobility in Canada and the United
States: a comparison.' *American Sociological Review* 46: 406-21.

Mah, Jay-Dell

1976 'Struggle for recognition.' *Canada and the World* 42: 16-17.

Mao, Tse-Tung

1967 *Selected Readings of Mao Tse-Tung*. Vol. II. Peking: Foreign
Language Press.

Miles, Robert

1982 *Racism and Migrant Labour*. London: Routledge and Kegan
Paul.

Miller, Robert
1977 'Unhyphenated Canadians.' *Maclean's* 90: 42b-p.

Milner, Sheilagh, and Henry Milner
1973 *The Decolonization of Quebec*. Toronto: McClelland and Stewart.

Montreal Star
1974 'Bride fights back tears as Chinese families reunited.' Aug. 26.

Morse, H. B.
1918 *The International Relations of the Chinese Empire*. Vol. II. London: Longmans, Green and Co.

Morton, James
1974 *In the Sea of Sterile Mountains: The Chinese in British Columbia*. Vancouver: J.J. Douglas.

Munro, John A.
1971 'British Columbia and the Chinese evil: Canada's first anti-Asiatic immigration law.' *Journal of Canadian Studies* 6: 42-51.

Nee, Victor G., and Brett de Bary Nee
1973 *Longtime Californ': A Documentary Study of an American Chinatown*. Boston: Houghton Mifflin Co.

New York Times
1974 'China letting 300 move to Canada.' April 25.

Palmer, Howard D.
1970 'Anti-Oriental sentiment in Alberta 1880-1920.' *Canadian Ethnic Studies* 11:31-57.

Parai, Louis
1965 *Immigration and Emigration of Professional and Skilled Manpower During the Post-war Period*. Special Study Number 1, Economic Council of Canada. Ottawa.

Park, Robert E.
1950 *Race and Culture*. Glencoe, Illinois: Free Press.

Pentland, H.C.
1959 'The development of a capitalistic labour market in Canada.' *Canadian Journal of Economics and Political Science* 25: 450-61.

Perkins, Dwight H.
1969 *Agricultural Development in China, 1368-1968*. Chicago: Aldine.

Porter, John
1965 *The Vertical Mosaic*. Toronto: Univ. of Toronto Press.

Purcell, Victor
1966 *The Chinese in Southeast Asia*. London: Oxford Univ. Press.

Ramu, G.N.
1976 'The Family and Marriage in Canada.' Pp. 295-348 in G.N. Ramu and S.D. Johnson, eds. *Introduction to Canadian Society*. Toronto: Macmillan.

Reitz, Jeffrey
1980   *The Survival of Ethnic Groups*. Toronto: McGraw-Hill Ryerson.
Rex, John
1983   *Race Relations in Sociological Theory*. 2d ed. London: Routledge and Kegan Paul.
Richmond, Anthony H. and Warren E. Kalbach
1980   *Factors in the Adjustment of Immigrants and Their Descendents*. Statistics Canada, Catalogue 99-761E.
Roberts, Lance and Rodney Clifton
1982   'Exploring the ideology of Canadian multiculturalism.' *Canadian Public Policy* 8: 88-94.
Rosen, Bernard C.
1956   'The achievement syndrome: a psychocultural dimension of social stratification.' *American Sociological Review* 21: 203-11.
1959   'Race, ethnicity and the achievement syndrome.' *American Sociological Review* 24: 47-60.
Roy, Patricia E.
1976   'The preservation of the peace in Vancouver: the aftermath of the anti-Chinese riot of 1887.' *BC Studies* 31: 45-59.
Satzewich, Victor, and Peter S. Li
1987   'Immigrant labour in Canada: the cost and benefit of ethnic origin in the job market.' *Canadian Journal of Sociology* 12: 229-41.
Saxton, Alexander
1971   *The Indispensable Enemy: Labor and Anti-Chinese Movement in California*. Berkeley and Los Angeles: Univ. of California Press.
Saywell, John Tupper
1951   'Labour and socialism in British Columbia: a survey of historical development before 1903.' *British Columbia Historical Quarterly* 15: 129-50.
Sedgwick, C.P., and W.E. Willmott
1974   'External influences and emerging identity: the evolution of community structure among Chinese Canadians.' *Canadian Forum* 54: 8-12.
Shibutani, Tamotsu, and Kian M. Kwan
1965   *Ethnic Stratification: A Comparative Approach*. New York: Macmillan.
Shurmann, Franz and Orville Schell, eds.
1967   *Imperial China*. New York: Vintage.
Siu, Paul C.P.
1953   'The sojourner.' *American Journal of Sociology* 58: 34-44.
Skinner, G. William
1957   *Chinese Society in Thailand: An Analytical History*. Ithaca, N.Y.: Cornell Univ. Press.

Stasiulis, Daiva K.
  1980 'The political structuring of ethnic community action: a
         reformulation.' *Canadian Ethnic Studies* 12: 19-44.
Steinberg, Stephen
  1981 *The Ethnic Myth*. Boston: Beacon Press.
Stewart, Watt
  1970 *Chinese Bondage in Peru: A History of the Chinese Coolie in Peru,
         1849-1874*. Westport, Conn.: Greenwood Press.
Sunahara, Ann Gomer
  1981 *The Politics of Racism: The Uprooting of Japanese Canadians
         During the Second World War*. Toronto: James Lorimer and Co.
Thernstrom, Stephan
  1977 *Poverty and Progress: Social Mobility in a Nineteenth Century
         City*. New York: Atheneum.
Timlin, Mable F.
  1960 'Canada's immigration policy, 1896-1910.' *Canadian Journal of
         Economics and Political Sciences* 26: 517-32.
Toronto Star
  1974 'Canada asked to let in 10,000 Chinese.' March 27.
  1984 'Chinese centre parking ''chaos'' draws ire of 500.' May 29.
Valentine, Charles A.
  1968 *Culture and Poverty*. Chicago: Univ. of Chicago Press.
Wagley, Charles and Marvin Harris
  1959 *Minorities in the New World*. New York: Columbia Univ. Press.
Wakeman, Frederic Jr.
  1975 *The Fall of Imperial China*. New York: Free Press.
Wallerstein, Immanuel
  1979 *The Capitalist World-Economy*. Cambridge: Cambridge Univ.
         Press.
Ward, Robin and Richard Jenkins, eds.
  1984 *Ethnic Communities in Business*. Cambridge: Cambridge Univ.
         Press.
Ward, W. Peter
  1974 'The oriental immigrant and Canada's Protestant clergy, 1858-
         1925.' *BC Studies* 22: 40-55.
  1978 *White Canada Forever*. Montreal: McGill-Queen's Univ. Press.
  1980 'Class and race in the social structure of British Columbia,
         1870-1939.' *BC Studies* 45: 17-35.
Wellman, David T.
  1977 *Portraits Of White Racism*. London: Cambridge Univ. Press.
Wickberg, Edgar
  1965 *The Chinese in Philippine Life*. New Haven: Yale Univ. Press.
  1979 'Some problems in Chinese organizational development in
         Canada, 1923-1937.' *Canadian Ethnic Studies* 11: 88-97.

1980   'Chinese and Canadian influences on Chinese politics in
        Vancouver, 1900-1947.' *BC Studies* 45: 37-55.
Williams, Robin W.
    1964   *Strangers Next Door*. Eaglewood Cliffs, N.J.: Prentice-Hall.
Willmott, Donald E.
    1960   *The Chinese in Semarang: A Changing Minority Community in
            Indonesia*. Ithaca, N.Y.: Cornell Univ. Press.
Willmott, William E.
    1964   'Chinese clan associations in Vancouver.' *Man* 64-5: 33-7.
    1967   *The Chinese in Cambodia*. Hong Kong: Cathay Press.
    1970   'Approaches to the study of the Chinese in British Columbia.'
            BC Studies 4: 38-52.
Woodsworth, Charles J.
    1941   *Canada and the Orient: A Study in International Relations*.
            Toronto: Macmillan.
Wright, Erik Olin
    1977   'Marxist class categories and income inequality.' *American
            Sociological Review* 42: 32-55.
    1978   'Race, class, and income inequality.' *American Journal of
            Sociology* 83: 1368-97.
    1979   *Class Structure and Income Determination*. New York: Academic
            Press.
Yancey, William L., E.P. Ericksen and R.N. Juliani
    1976   'Emergent ethnicity: a review and reformation.' *American
            Sociological Review* 41: 391-403.

Author Index

Subject Index